ON YOUR DORESTEP

25 walks in and around Dore

by

David Bearpark
David Heslop
Roger Millican

With additional material by John Dunstan

Dore Village Society

ON YOUR DORESTEP

25 walks in and around Dore

by
David Bearpark
David Heslop
Roger Millican

With additional material by John Dunstan

ISBN 978-0-9500461-2-9

Dore Village Society
8 Thornsett Gardens
Sheffield S17 3PP

Printed in the UK by the University of Sheffield Print Service

ACKNOWLEDGEMENTS

When the authors agreed to write a walking book on behalf of the Dore Village Society, we thought that it would be straightforward – after all, we all enjoy walking and know local walks. It was as we were discussing and planning the book that we started to realise what we had taken on; and as the months passed, we became even more aware of the scale of the task, especially as we were determined to produce a quality book.

If we have achieved our objective, it has been in no small measure due to the help and assistance we have received from a variety of Dore residents, all on a voluntary basis.

We would like to start by recording our thanks to the individuals who initially walked each walk, sometimes in adverse weather, and produced the first drafts for each walk. These are: John Baker, Julie Bearpark, Sally and Garry Carter, Philip Hetherington, Susan and John Robinson, Sue and David Ward and Fiona and Stephen Willetts. However, each walk was walked for a final time by one of the authors and any mistakes that remain are their responsibility.

We wanted to produce a walking book that, as well as detailing interesting walks, also gave some detail to features along the way and some historical background. For this aspect of the book we need to thank John Dunstan who has used his extensive local background and interest in these matters to produce a series of excellent potted summaries, which we believe add significantly to the book and which we hope will add to the enjoyment of it by its users. John also undertook the demanding task of compiling the index, as well as providing the comprehensive information regarding public transport options for the walks.

The book is also graced by a number of first-class photographs showing landmarks and views in the areas of the walks. For these we thank John Doornkamp. Many of the users of the book will also recognise David Heslop's delightful illustrations.

Any publication needs detailed proof reading to spot inconsistencies, grammatical issues and general mistakes. Assistance with proof reading has been provided by Chris Cave, John Dunstan and Philip Hetherington; and we would like to thank them for their attention to detail. If any errors remain, they are the sole responsibility of the authors.

In conclusion, we hope that all who use this book enjoy both the walks contained within it and the supporting background notes. We hope it encourages people to walk more – and not just the walks in this book.

1st August 2008

WALKING

There is nothing like walking to get the feel of the country. A fine landscape is like a piece of music; it must be taken at the right tempo. Even a bicycle goes too fast.
Paul Scott Mowrer

In every walk with nature one receives far more than he seeks.
John Muir

If you are seeking creative ideas, go out walking. Angels whisper to a man when he goes for a walk.
Raymond Inmon

My father considered a walk among the mountains as the equivalent of churchgoing.
Aldous Huxley

Walking is the great adventure, the first meditation, a practice of heartiness and soul primary to humankind. Walking is the exact balance between spirit and humility.
Gary Snyder

Slow down and enjoy life. It's not only the scenery you miss by going fast – you also miss the sense of where you are going and why.
Eddie Cantor

CONTENTS

Colour key

Start and finish in Dore
Start or finish not in Dore
Start and finish elsewhere

Longshaw in winter

FOREWORD

In these days of wide ranging and rapid travel, it is all too easy to miss the beauty and interest on one's own doorstep. So wherever you live, it is worth taking a break to explore the area around you, and there can be no better or healthier way than to do this on foot.

Sheffield is reputed to be the greenest city in England, and Dore, on its fringes, lives up to this claim, surrounded as it is by green farmland and ancient woodland. Sitting in a natural bowl surrounded by hills, the immediate area is rich in natural and man made heritage dating from the Iron Age through to the beginnings of the industrial revolution. It also abuts the Peak District National Park, putting a wide range of different landscapes and historical sites within easy reach.

This book sets out to introduce you to the local diversity on offer, mainly with circular walks, most around the 5 to 6 mile range, but with some shorter urban strolls and a few more challenging excursions.

Time to put on those walking shoes and as the title says, explore *ON YOUR DORESTEP.*

John Baker
Chairman
Dore Village Society

INTRODUCTION

Just a few words of explanation about this book and its use.

DISTANCES: We have used metric scale throughout as the basis, with imperial conversions shown for longer distances. For shorter distances, assume metres and yards are approximately equal.

TIMES: The times shown are for walking at a moderate pace with a few short stops 'to gather one's breath' and admire the scenery. You should add further time for anticipated meal breaks or other prolonged stops.

TERRAIN: We have given a brief description of the terrain for each walk. This will include, if necessary, a warning about any arduous sections.

PUBLIC TRANSPORT: Where appropriate, each walk contains some information about the train and buses that can be used, either to get to or from the start and finish location or to reduce the walking distance. Due to seasonal and other changes, we strongly recommend that you check the service times before starting the walk either by contacting Traveline (01709 515151) or travelsouthyorkshire.com. At the time of writing (2008), the services shown in the table opposite may be of help.

REFRESHMENTS: Locations for refreshments are listed but we cannot guarantee that each one is open daily.

ROUTE INSTRUCTIONS: These have been written so that each walk can be done without the need to refer to an OS or similar map. However, you may wish to carry such a map as a backup. The letters at the start of each section match those on the sketch maps. Brackets have been used to denote names of roads and other features that are not apparent when first mentioned in the walk on the walk. Names without brackets should be visible immediately.

SKETCH MAPS: These have been included to provide a general idea of where each walk goes. You can also use them to follow progress during the walk.

INTEREST ITEMS: For each walk we have included some items of interest. These go some way to explain features, visible or lost, close to the walk route and, we hope, make your walks more interesting and enjoyable. Because some sections of the routes are duplicated on different walks, you may find further information on another walk. We gave up trying to cross-reference them!

PUBLIC TRANSPORT

Train
Sheffield-Manchester via Dore, Grindleford and Hathersage.

Buses

14 Chesterfield-Holmesfield via Dronfield (M-Sa)
30 Sheffield-Dore
65 Sheffield-Buxton via Dore Moor Inn
84 Sheffield-Ringinglow circular (M-F) (+)
89 Sheffield-Holmesfield via Millthorpe
97 Sheffield-Totley
98 Sheffield-Totley Brook (*)
213 Sheffield-Matlock via Totley (M-Sa)
214 Sheffield-Matlock via Dore Moor Inn
218 Sheffield-Bakewell/Buxton via Totley
240 Sheffield-Bakewell via Dore Moor Inn
272 Sheffield-Castleton via Hathersage
284 Sheffield-Hathersage via Ringinglow and Stanage (Summer Su & BH only))
293 Sheffield-Chesterfield via Abbeydale and Dronfield (M-Sa)
M17 Jordanthorpe-Dore via Bradway (M-Sa)

(*) To get to Dore, take the 98 to Furniss Avenue (stop before terminus), continue uphill to the T-junction and turn right.
(+) Up Long Line am, down pm.

DORE VILLAGE - A BUGGY WALK

Intended mainly for newcomers to Dore, this short buggy walk provides an introduction to some of the historical buildings and locations in the village - and a reason for a bit of exercise!

DISTANCE 3½km (2¼ miles)

MINIMUM TIME 1½ hours

TERRAIN Mainly pavements and roads. A few inclines

LANDSCAPE Suburban but with distant views of woods and moors

START/FINISH Old School, Dore

PARKING On road in Dore

PUBLIC TOILETS None on route

REFRESHMENTS Two pubs (Devonshire Arms and Hare & Hounds) and a cafe in the village

TRAINS & BUSES Services 30, 98 and M17

As many of our walks start from the Old School, let's have a look at its history.

DORE OLD SCHOOL: The Old School building dates from the mid-18th century when the originally self-contained section next to Savage Lane provided a schoolroom plus accommodation for the master. Extensions to the back followed in the 1770s-80s. Then the 1809 Dore Enclosure Act set up a Trust to fund the school from land rents. The plaque Erected by Subscription AD 1821 applies to the front door and the southern range continuing on its left (except for the later end bay, which explains why the plaque isn t central). The famous Richard Furness presided here from 1821 to 1848. The present western range on Vicarage Lane was begun in 1863 as an infant school . More housing for teachers was added to this, only to be converted into further space for the infants in 1878. Thus, more or less, it stayed until 1965, when the children were transferred to the new school off Furniss Avenue. It was restored in the early 1970s for community use and enlarged and refurbished to mark the millennium. For much, much more, see our *Dore Old School in Records and Recollections* (DVS, 2006).

Route Directions

Start by enjoying the view from the car park: from right to left, the Old School, the War Memorial and the King Ecgbert Stone on the Green. **See King Ecgbert Stone.**

KING ECGBERT STONE: Also known as the Dore Stone, this was planned by the Dore Village Society, designed by R. Elden Minns, financed by Sheffield City Council and unveiled following the 1968 Well Dressing Service by the Lord Mayor. The sandstone block is from Stoke Hall, Grindleford. The plaque of black Scottish granite represents a Saxon shield. The wyvern, which purists say is two legs short of dragonhood, is the emblem of Ecgbert and Wessex. The small red emblem at the base (a cross between four leopards) stands for Northumbria.

A Leave the Old School yard by the large gateway and turn right (Savage Lane) and then almost immediately turn left into Vicarage Lane. Have a look at the Stone on the Village Green. Continue along Vicarage Lane past the Old Vicarage of 1841 and two rather

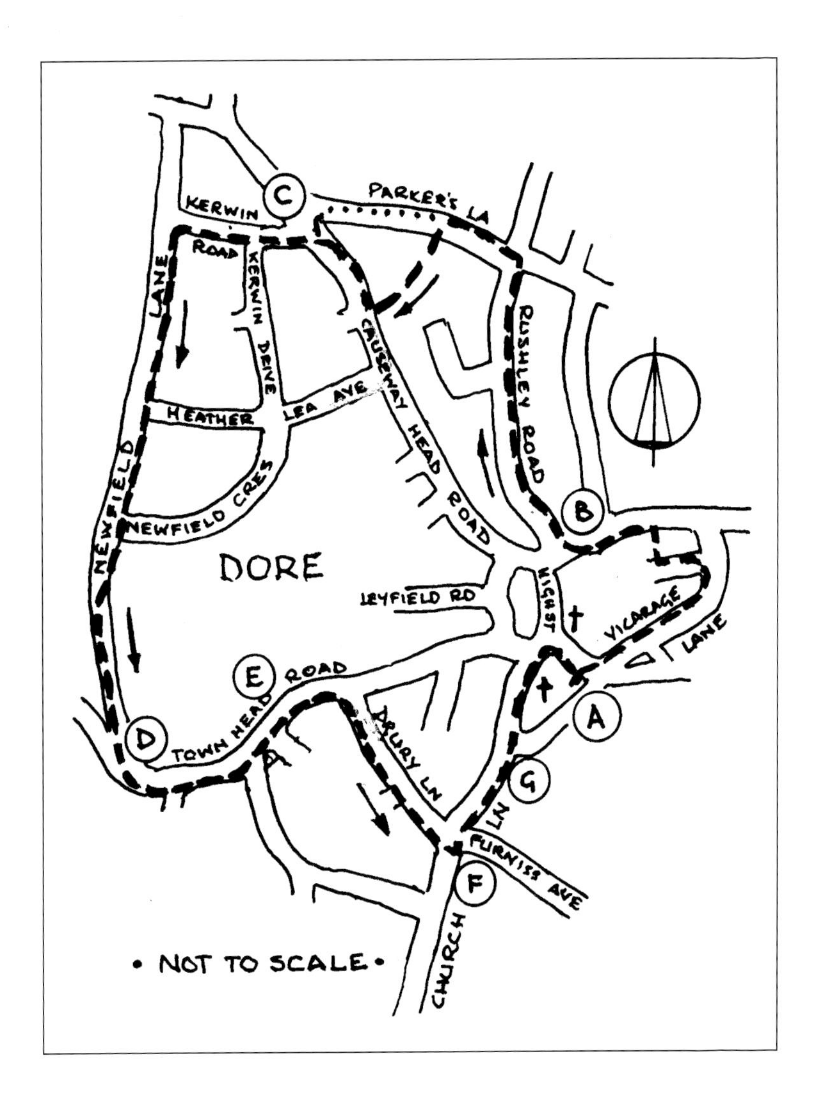

The Hornbeam leaf and fruit

rare hornbeams - yielding our hardest timber - rounding the bend and turning left up Dore Hall Croft. **See Dore Hall.**

At the top, find a footpath by a telephone pole, and descend it to the road (Dore Road). Cross the road and turn left up the rise. Opposite Rushleigh Court flats, where the grass verge narrows, look back to view what is left of Hall Green (the widest part of the grass verge opposite Vicarage Lane), the best preserved of Dore's six greens after the Village Green.

DORE HALL: You are standing on the site of Dore Hall Farm, demolished in 1964. Dore Hall was the home of the Barker family, from the 14th century until the early 18th. It was well past its glory days by 1744 when absentee owner Sir Robert Barker sold his small estate (35.6ha, 88 acres) to the Duke of Devonshire, the new lord of the manor. Stone from it was recycled in other local properties such as The Grange up Dore Road, and its last remains were cleared in 1840.

B Then, passing The Grange on your left, turn second right into Rushley Road. **See Rushley.**

RUSHLEY: Rushley probably means a rushy meadow. Trees behind No. 42 help to locate Rushley Farm, vanished seat of the Hancock family, once leading citizens of Dore. Their name was given to a new street, only to be supplanted by Rushley Drive . A ganister miner at Limb Pits is said to have brought up his 13 children in Rushley Cottage, long before it was extended. Dore s Victorian sexton, Joe Parker, lived near here in Parkers Lane.

Near the top of this road, a cluster of five trees on the right marks the former entrance of long-gone Rushley Farm. Note Rushley Cottage opposite, in part 17th century. Whirlow comes into view ahead. At the cross roads turn left into Parkers Lane. To the right are views of Whirlow Brook Park and Standhills, and straight ahead Lady Canning's Plantation. Just after the road bends to the left, a footpath sign appears on the left. If you have a buggy or pram, ignore the sign and continue to Causeway Head Road.

Otherwise take the footpath, along the left of two parallel drives. You should see a garage numbered 22. Enter a path on the right of the garage to reach a stile. On the top are the words PEACE MADE. Cross the stile, turn right, then right again into Causeway Head Road, then second left into Kerwin Road. **See Causeway Head.**

CAUSEWAY HEAD: Crossing the stile and passing the Peace Stone (1856), you are in the ancient hamlet of Causeway Head or Causeyhead, literally on the edge of the moors until the Dore Enclosure Act was implemented in 1822. Till then they actually extended to and beyond part of Limb Lane. Regular rectangular fields were typical of the new allotments . A copy of the Dore Enclosure map can be seen in the DVS office.

If you have emerged from Parkers Lane direct into Causeway Head Road, turn left and then right into Kerwin Road. If you want to see the Peace Stone, make a short detour further along Causeway Head Road to the footpath sign on the left and go down the lane to the stile, then retracing your steps to Kerwin Road.

C In Kerwin Road, continue to the T-junction at the far end. Ahead, beyond a distant house with static caravans, Houndkirk Moor can be seen on the horizon. Turn left into Newfield Lane. Soon you pass the distinctive arched double lodges of Dore Moor House. **See Dore Moor House.** Where the pavement ends, at the entrance to St Catherine's, cross the road to face oncoming traffic. Glimpse the moors through the trees on the right.

D At the foot of Newfield Lane are benches with fine views of the hills and moors. Blacka dominates in the centre with Houndkirk on the right, Totley Moor on the left and Owler Bar on the far left horizon. Now turn left into Townhead Road, taking great care as the corner is blind. Listen for traffic from all directions including Whitelow Lane behind you. The pavement resumes at Knowle Green, commemorating another of Dore's ancient greens along the roadside.

DORE MOOR HOUSE: Dore Moor House, now several properties, was probably the grandest in Dore. It was designed by A.F. Royds, a pupil of the famous Edwin Lutyens, and built in 1906 for W.J. Armitage, a director of Brown Bayley s steelworks. Sir Allan J. Grant of Firth Brown s lived here during World War II. Its site is the New Field despite its name an ancient 17th century enclosure from the commons hence New field Lane.

E At the top of the rise is Townhead. **See Townhead**. Pass a row of small cottages on the left, then Cromwell Cottages with the datestone RW 1686 over the door of No. 88. A short distance ahead, turn right into Drury Lane The grassy area at the junction is known as The Cockpit.

TOWNHEAD: The two Cromwell Cottages originally formed a single substantial dwelling, probably built by yeoman farmer Robert Woodhouse. Within living memory this had become three cottages, latterly two. The undocumented name is 30 years too late for the Civil War, but the 8 of 1686 does resemble a 5. The Cockpit evokes an ancient spectator sport common two centuries ago. Drury Lane recalls an ordinary Victorian family living here. Was it a bit of a joke name, thanks to its famous London counterpart?

The Cockpit

Christ Church

Keep to the right-hand side of Drury Lane as there is no pavement – though visibility is good – until Overdale Gardens.

F At the cross roads, turn left and cross Church Lane, pausing to look westwards. The grass verge is modern but serves as a symbol of Oxen Green which stretched all the way to the far corner. Cross Furniss Avenue and continue along Church Lane to the village centre. Christ Church soon comes into view. **See Christ Church.**

CHRIST CHURCH: Christ Church was built in 1829 as a chapel-of-ease for Dore and Totley, replacing a dilapidated building at the corner of Church Lane and Savage Lane. Schoolmaster Richard Furness had a big hand in drawing up the specification and supervising the work. At the same time Dore acquired its graveyard, but had to wait until 1843 to achieve parochial independence from Dronfield. The choir vestry was completed by 1881, the chancel by 1896 and the vicar s vestry by 1932.

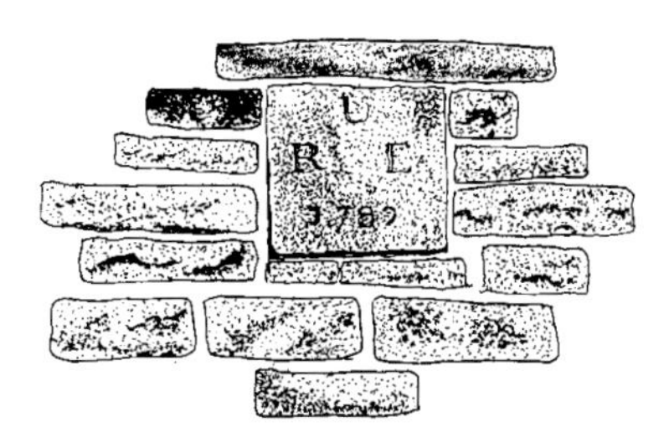

Datestone, Cobblers Row, Savage Lane

G Pause just before crossing Vicarage Lane to your right. Here was Catty Croft Green, now tiny and mostly tarmac. Note some very old buildings: Church Lane Farm on the right preserves a former name of this section of Vicarage Lane, while parts of the Croft House Farm barn on the left go back 500-600 years. Continue along Church Lane, passing the Hare & Hounds to make a final historical stop at the corner. **See Dore Village Centre.** Turn right down Savage Lane to the Old School, noting the datestone on the cottage on the left

DORE VILLAGE CENTRE: Where High Street and Church Lane cross Townhead Road and Savage Lane is the ancient hub of Dore, from the days when the bridleway from Sheffield to Holmesfield and beyond crossed one from Norton to Hathersage. Canons from Beauchief probably set up the preaching cross discovered on the site of the first Christian chapel. The pubs are both 18th century. The Methodist church started in 1861 as a Primitive (i.e. original) Methodist chapel. Since turned at a right angle, it has a splendid stained-glass window and its radio-controlled Millennium clock should always be accurate. The datestone on the Savage Lane cottages, once Cobblers Row, refers to Robert and Elizabeth Unwin in 1782.

Cottages, Savage Lane

TOWNHEAD AND OLDHAY, DORE

This walk offers a wealth of features: beautiful and varied views of moors, woods and farmland, and a number of sites recalling the area's important industrial past.

DISTANCE	4¼km (2½ miles)
MINIMUM TIME	1½ hours
TERRAIN	Mainly paths and pavement but a stretch through fields
LANDSCAPE	Good views of countryside around the village
START/FINISH	The Old School, Dore
PARKING	On road in Dore
PUBLIC TOILETS	None on route
REFRESHMENTS	Two pubs (Devonshire Arms and Hare & Hounds) and a cafe in Dore, Crown Inn near Oldhay (off route)
TRAINS & BUSES	Bus services 30, 98 and M17

Route Directions

A Leave the Old School car park via the large gateway (Savage Lane), turn left to walk up to the road junction, there turn left in front of the Hare & Hounds and then immediately right into Townhead Road. **See Farm Cottage.**

FARM COTTAGE (38 TOWNHEAD ROAD): Farm Cottage (38 Townhead Road) was the home of Elisha Parker, saw grinder, farmer, postmaster and principal victim of the Dore Outrages. He refused to leave a firm employing two non-union men. In 1853-4 his horse was hamstrung, his household nearly got blown up, and he was shot in the arm and permanently disabled. Saw Grinders Union secretary William Broadhead rewarded the hamstringers and paid for Parker s assailant to emigrate to America. A controversial figure, Broadhead somehow obtained a certificate of indemnity.

Pass the Post Office on the left and Dore Parish Church Hall on the right, ignoring the footpath sign alongside the Church Hall and, shortly after passing Drury Lane on your left, turn right at the Recreation Ground signpost.

Cottage, Townhead Road

Continue on the path across the recreation ground at first and then between garden fences to meet Newfield Crescent.

B Turn right and, at the next cross roads, turn left up Heather Lea Avenue. Continue ahead to meet Newfield Lane at a T-junction, with views of woods and open moors

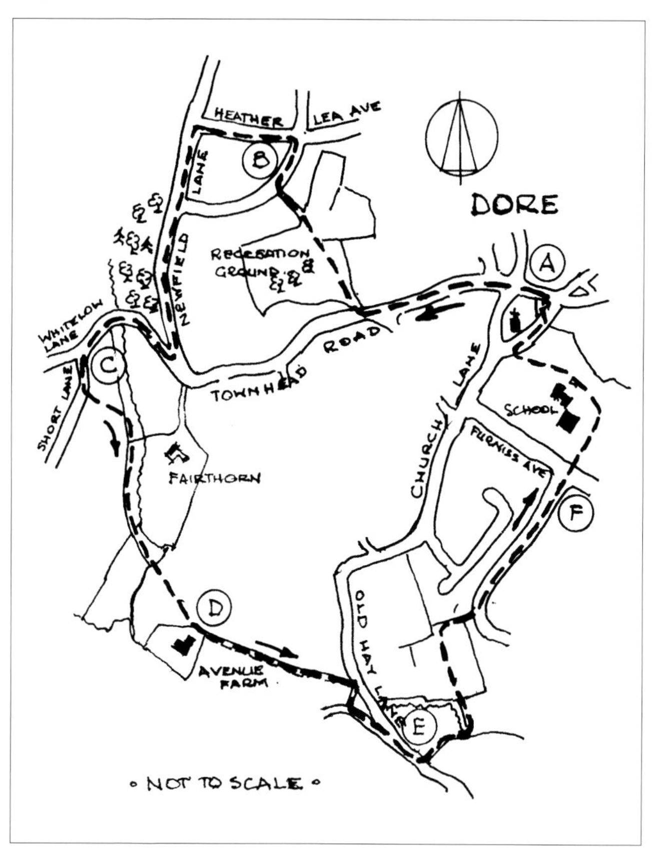

ahead. Turn left and keep on this lane, soon with woodland on your right, for about 300m until you reach a crossing road with 30 mph signs to your left. *Fairthorn, which provides housing with care, is along the lane ahead.* **See Fairthorn.**

Turn right here, down Whitelow Lane, taking care as there is no pavement. Wag Wood is on your right. **See Wag Wood.** After crossing the brook (Redcar Brook), continue uphill for 100m then turn left into Shorts Lane. **See Shorts Lane.**

FAIRTHORN: Late in the 19th century a group of Sheffield teachers organized a holiday home at Redmires for children from the east end of the city. In the early 1930s this had to be vacated. So the Fairthorn site was bought and the house built, opening in 1934. It was modernized over the years but the need for it gradually decreased. In 1971 the Home Farm Trust acquired it. It changed hands again and has now been converted into superior flats for elderly people.

WAG WOOD: Wag Wood and the cottage take their name from a family of lead smelters who rented a mill upstream from the bridge early in the 18th century. Recorded from 1617 until 1739, it was known as the Upper Mill at Dore Town End, presumably to distinguish it from the other Upper Mill below Oldhay. It was then turned into Town End Cupola, already ruinous by 1811. There seems to have been a second lead mill near here, Cliff Mill, operating briefly around 1670.

C After 90m and where the lane bends slightly to the right, turn left at a footpath sign, crossing a wall and then a wooden stile immediately after.

SHORTS LANE: Shorts Lane or Short Lane, with passionate advocates in 1968 when the Council sign appeared is reputedly named after an old man who lived here. Nearing the stile, look back to where you were: perhaps you can see traces of an ancient bridleway coming down across the slope from Fairthorn towards the brook. This preceded Whitelow Lane, an enclosure road. The field opposite the stile has the misleading name Bread Doles, once Bredy Dole, portion of land by the gushing stream .

In a few metres turn right through a gate, with a stile on its right, and follow the direction of the footpath arrow to go diagonally down the field to the far left corner. Go through a gap in the wall and continue in the same diagonal direction to reach a wooden stile in the tree and hedge boundary of the field. Another stile follows in quick succession.

Christ Church, Dore

Bearing right, continue on the path with the stream on your left, and just before the track reaches a ford, turn right over a wooden stile, and after 20m cross a wooden footbridge over the stream on your left. Turn slightly right and walk in the direction of a large house ahead to cross a fence stile into another field and then continue to meet the metalled drive at Avenue Farm. **See Avenue Farm & Oldhay.**

D Turn left along the drive, with a very neat wall on the left, and soon a brook (Oldhay Brook) is visible on your right. In this area is a weir associated with the old millponds and water wheels. Continue along this drive to meet a road (Old Hay Lane).

Immediately before the road, turn right at a public footpath sign through a gate between stone pillars on to a path that goes down flagstone steps and over a footbridge to a metalled track. Ahead of you here is a large wooded mound made from spoil dug from the construction of the nearby Totley Tunnel. Turn left and on reaching the road turn right. After 150m, and soon after the brow of a little rise, turn left over a stone stile on to a signed footpath.

AVENUE FARM & OLDHAY: Near Avenue Farm a paper mill was operating in 1721 and possibly in 1650. In the 1830s it was a forge for manufacturing scythe blades and the two concerns became one. Totley Forge became Tyzack s Forge and Joshua Tyzack converted it into Avenue Farm in 1891. A short distance downstream, Oldhay was a major industrial site. A big lead smelting mill was at work by 1585 and continued until early in the 19th century. Later it was a scythe grinding wheel.

E Continue on this path, with a high wall on the right, pass through a metal kissing gate and over a footbridge. Here was another mill site, Upper Mill.

Almost immediately, where the wall bends sharply to the right, cross another footbridge to your left. From the bridge continue straight ahead on the path curving up to some stone steps and a gap in the wall. Continue ahead up the path in the middle of the field, and 30m after passing a bench on your left turn right onto a tarmac path towards a gap between the houses. On meeting a road (Totley Brook Road) bear left uphill and walk past bus stops and the entrance to King Ecgbert School to a T-junction (Furniss Avenue).

F Cross Furniss Avenue to walk directly ahead on a surfaced footpath with lamp-posts on its left. A few metres after passing the path to the primary school on your left turn left, walking gently uphill up a green open space with a row of trees on your left. Towards the top of this open space bear left through the trees to reach the footpath adjacent to the school's metal fence. Continue up the footpath alongside the fence to meet Vicarage Lane, with Dore Church directly ahead. Turn right and after 100m arrive at the Old School.

Church Lane Farm, Vicarage Lane

The former Mercia site of King Ecgbert's School in winter. At the time writing (2008), the site is the subject of a contested planning application for housing.

POYNTON WOOD AND TOTLEY

An easy walk but with plenty of local interest, it will take you to places that otherwise may be missed.
Ideal for a summer evening or a Sunday afternoon.

DISTANCE	5km (3 miles)
MINIMUM TIME	2 hours, and that's being generous
TERRAIN	Good paths and pavements
LANDSCAPE	Woodland and urban but with good views of Blacka Moor
START/FINISH	The Old School, Dore
PARKING	On road in Dore
PUBLIC TOILETS	None on route
REFRESHMENTS	Two pubs (Devonshire Arms and Hare & Hounds) and a cafe in Dore, Seasons cafe on Abbeydale Road South and Cricket Inn. Diversions to Cross Scythes, Fleur de Lys and Crown Inn in Totley also possible
TRAINS & BUSES	Bus services 30, 98 and M17

Route Directions

A Using the large gateway, turn right out of the Old School car park and, after 30m, turn left at the crossroads to keep the Village Green and King Ecgbert Stone on your right. This is Vicarage Lane and you will pass Sycamore Cottage on your right and the Old Vicarage on your left. After about 250m, turn right at the public footpath sign through a kissing gate. Follow the tarmac path downhill passing the allotments on your left. At the road (Burlington Grove) turn left and after 80m turn right at another public footpath sign. Continue ahead and cross a drive but keep descending the signed footpath to a road (Ashfurlong Road).

Cavendish Avenue in autumn

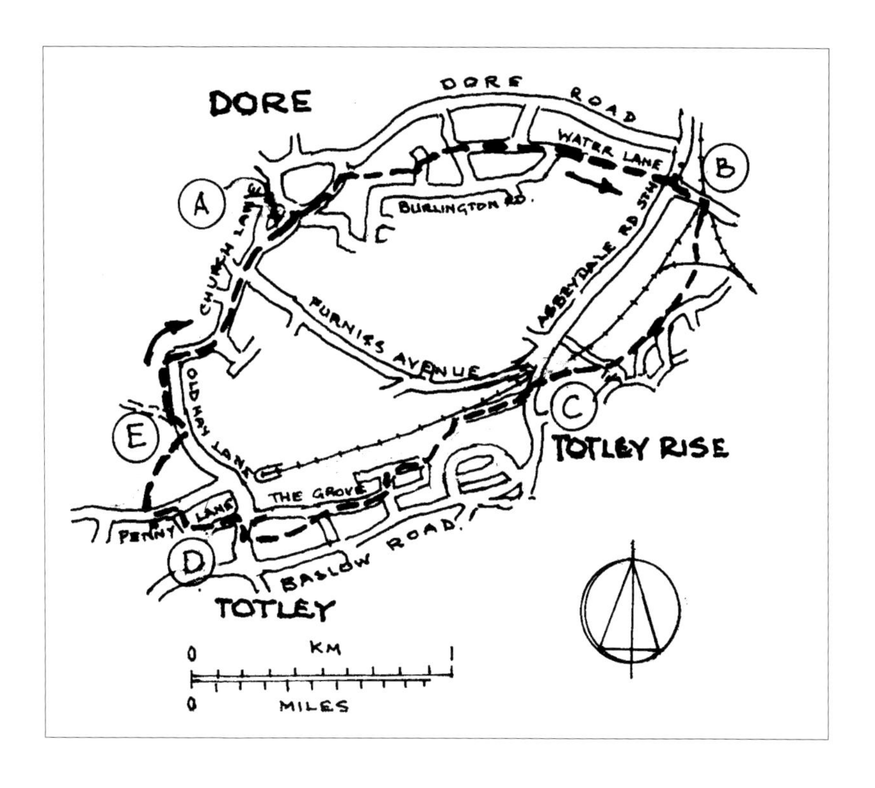

Then keep straight ahead down to the lower end of Cavendish Avenue. Where Ashfurlong Road appears again on your right, keep straight on. A few metres into this road, bear right to follow the footpath which runs parallel to and on the right of the public bridleway. This is Water Lane. You will now get good views of Abbeydale Sports Club on your right.

B At the main road take care as you cross and walk up Twentywell Lane ahead. **See Dore & Totley Station.** Cross over the River Sheaf and railway bridge, then immediately turn right at the public footpath sign and over a stile. Climb the track up the hill diagonally to your left, observing a cycle assault course on your right.

DORE & TOTLEY STATION: Latterly just Dore Station but recently regaining its old name, this was built in 1872 on the 2-year-old Sheffield and Chesterfield line. The lower part of Twentywell Lane has been much disturbed by successive railway works. Just before entering the footpath beyond the bridge, you pass on your left the site of the buildings of Walk Mill, dating from about 1280 and part of Beauchief Abbey s clothmaking enterprise. After the Dissolution it saw various edge-tool manufactures, with a 19th century interlude as a paper mill.

At the fence below the brow of the hill, the path sweeps to the right and enters woodland (Poynton Wood). Follow the path with the fence on your right. Climb the short slope and soon keep directly ahead on the upper of two paths as it moves away from the fence on your right and through the centre of the wood, climbing gradually. After about 200m, at a junction of paths, continue straight ahead on the right hand path looking down to the railway line, Totley Freight Loop, in the bottom of the valley.

In about another 300m, at another junction of paths, take the lower route between two trees ignoring the left hand steeper path. Follow this largely level and narrow path, ignoring another path on your left, and in 100m keep straight on ignoring a ravine path down to your right. In a further 80m bear right and follow the path downhill with houses above on your left. Pass over a crossing concrete path and descend with blocks of flats on your right, crossing a small wooden bridge and then a hand-railed bridge over a small stream and weir. Continue up the short lane past Mill Cottage on your left, turning right on a short path before the junction of the lane with the main road.

C Cross the main road at the bus stop. Go straight ahead down Grove Road with the Methodist Church on your left. **See Totley Rise Methodist Church.**

TOTLEY RISE METHODIST CHURCH: In August 1881 local preachers from the Sheffield Brunswick Wesleyan Methodist Circuit held an open air service at Totley Rise and cottage meetings began in September. Over a decade later, with a spurt in population growth, the congregation decided to raise funds to build a chapel. Land was donated by Ebenezer Hall of Abbeydale Hall and the chapel opened early in 1896. A new Sunday School followed in 1931. Both buildings were extended in 1958, and the church greatly enlarged in 1991.

At a footbridge on your right divert a moment to observe Totley Tunnel East signal box, then return to the road and cross straight over following a path, which shortly bears right with Oldhay Brook on its left.

Totley Tunnel East signal box

Cross the bridge on the left at a weir and climb the path through woodland (Akley Bank). When you arrive at a road (The Quadrant) turn right, then next left into Terrey Road, then right again into The Grove. Continue along getting rare aerial views of King Ecgbert School between the houses and bungalows on the right. At the end of the road turn left along a fenced path and at the old gateposts where this meets a crossing road (Butts Hill), turn right. This brings you to a road junction opposite Totley All Saints School. **See Totley All Saints School.**

TOTLEY ALL SAINTS SCHOOL: Totley s first school was built in 1826 on the initiative of D Ewes Coke Jr. It was superintended by the incumbent of Dore and Totley and can still be seen in Totley Hall Lane. The 1870 Education Act led to a big drive to get all children into schools. This was tackled in Totley by opening a larger school: Totley Church School moved to its present site in 1877. Its story was published in 2000 by Joan Stratford, a former head.

D Turn right here down Hillfoot Road, then immediately on your left stop to visit The Pinfold Garden. Now turn left following the public footpath sign down Chapel Lane through a gap stile and down a cobbled path. As the path levels out you cross over a stream, then reach a lane.

Cobbled path, Penny Lane

Turn left up the lane (Penny Lane) and pass the Cricket Inn on your left and Lower Bents Farm, an English Heritage listed building, on your right, before turning right at the public footpath sign. Pass Swallow Cottage on your left and follow the footpath sign by turning right through a gate opposite the farm buildings. Go over a stone stile and turn left along the left hand edge of a field. Cross another stile at the edge of a house wall before descending some steps and walking down the drive of the house. After passing the second house, named Old Hay, with an old gas lamp by its gate, turn left up a path, climb the steps and through a gate to a road.

E Turn left up the road, ignoring the drive to Avenue Farm, and then immediately go left again over a stone stile. Climb the right hand edge of the field, to a stile in the top right hand corner. Then walk straight ahead along the road (no footpath for about 100m). In about 400m, just before the church, turn right along Vicarage Lane and back to the Old School.

Lower Bents Farm

THRYFT HOUSE AND LIMB VALLEY

At Firs Farm on this walk you will get one of the best panoramic views in the area covering moorland to the west, the Don Valley to the east and the Sheaf Valley to the south. Go find it!

DISTANCE	7¼km (4½ miles)
MINIMUM TIME	2¼ hours
TERRAIN	Good paths mainly, one steep climb and one section could be a bit boggy after wet weather – but not bad
LANDSCAPE	Excellent distant views in many directions
START/FINISH	Ecclesall Woods car park, Limb Lane (the continuation of Rushley Road), Dore
PARKING	At the car park
PUBLIC TOILETS	None on route
REFRESHMENTS	Two pubs (Devonshire Arms and Hare & Hounds) and a cafe in Dore, Whirlow Brook Hall (hours vary) and W.O.R.K.
TRAINS & BUSES	Not served direct by bus. Bus services 30, 83, 84, 98, 284 and M17 may be helpful.

Route Directions

The initial directions are provided for those who may wish to start the walk at the Old School in Dore village.

Leave the Old School yard by the large gateway, cross the road (Savage Lane) and turn left. Walk up towards the village centre. At the junction (High Street) turn right, passing the Methodist Church on the right and the Devonshire Arms on the left, and soon reach a staggered crossroads. Continue ahead into Rushley Road and follow this road, which becomes Limb Lane, for about 800m to reach the Ecclesall Woods car park.

A Leave the car park by the road entrance, turn right along Limb Lane and, after 100m, right again on the public bridleway signed to Abbeydale Road South. After about 400m enter Ecclesall Woods and then pass Ryecroft Glen Cottage.

Ryecroft Glen Cottage

50m after passing the cottage, turn left by a large gate on to a path signed to Whirlow. Passing over a number of small wooden plank bridges, continue

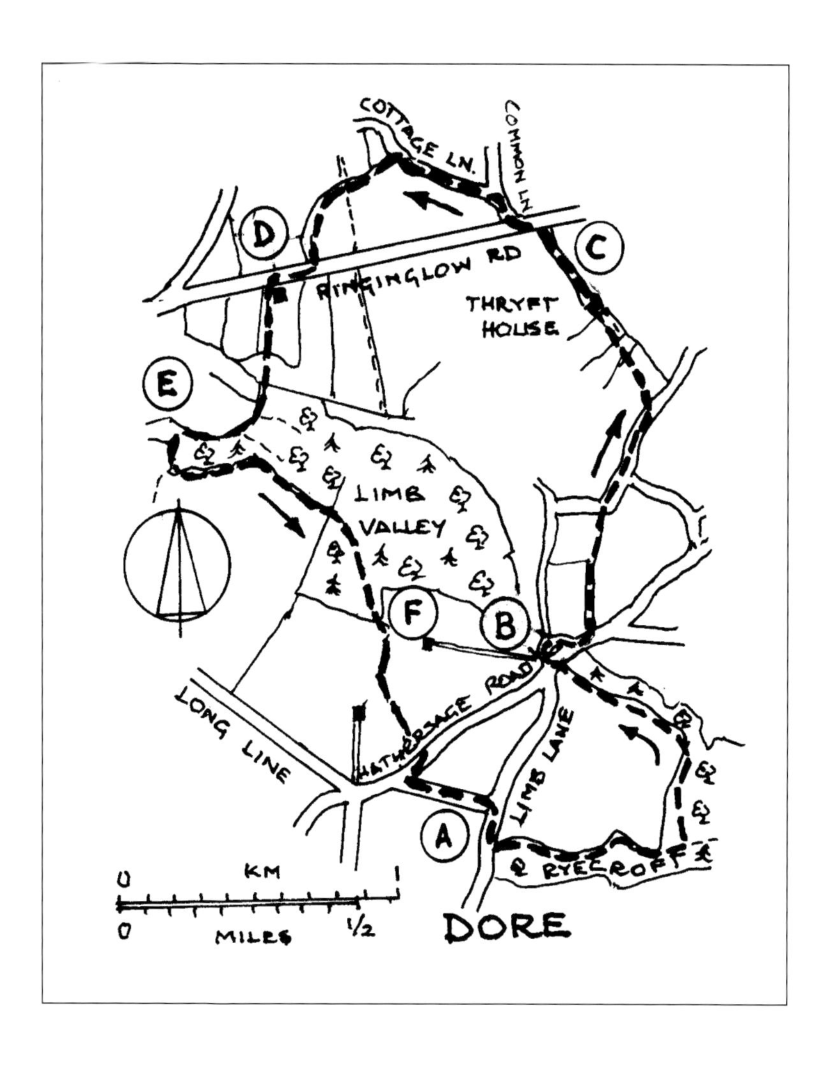

for about 400m to a junction of paths, where you take the left option, again signed to Whirlow.

This soon leads through a wall, where you should continue ahead up the right hand side of playing fields for about 500m, with a brook (Limb Brook) babbling away down to the right. At the top, bear left following a short section of track to join Limb Lane. Turn right here and cross the main road (Ecclesall Road South).

B Turn right and then immediately swing left to follow the section of the old road to pass the entrances to Whirlow Brook Park and Whinfell Quarry Garden. Continue on to pass the end of Whinfell Court and then, about 60m past the first bus stop, turn left up a signed public footpath between walls. Follow this for 500m to join a road (Broad Elms Lane) on a bend.

To the left is Whirlow Hall Farm with its farm shop (limited opening days).

Turn right and continue for about 400m, passing the end of Whirlow Lane and rising steadily. At the highest point, turn left through a gate and take the path diagonally right across the field. This continues through a number of gates for about 400m, eventually to reach a tarmac lane.

Turn left, passing Thryft House on the right and continue ahead for 300m to meet a road (Ringinglow Road). **See Thryft House.**

Refreshments are available six days a week at W.O.R.K., a centre providing training for adults with learning difficulties. To get there, turn right and, after 100m, cross the road and follow the signs past the right hand side of apartments. Retrace your steps afterwards.

THRYFT HOUSE: Thryft (or Thrift) House, Whirlow s historian Shirley Frost tells us, lay on the ancient packhorse route from the Baslow district, Dore, Fenney Lane and Whirlow Hall via what became Ringinglow Road and Psalter Lane to Sheffield. The house s name was cited in a lease of 1504, an unusually early date. About 1686 it was downgraded to a barn when a new house was built alongside. In 1883, when after a rebuilding of 1840 this was enlarged, the great thickness of the innermost walls revealed its origins.

C Turn left and, after 80m, turn right into Common Lane and continue for a further 150m before bearing left into Cottage Lane. Passing Whiteley Wood Cottage, continue for 350m where, on a right hand curve, you should take the second of two paths on the left. **See Cottage Lane School.**

Follow this alongside a wire fence, keeping the fields on the left throughout, until it meets a road (Ringinglow Road). Turn right and, walking close to the wall on the right, continue for about 150m, passing Firs Farm, before crossing the road and taking the stile on the left.

COTTAGE LANE SCHOOL: This building, marked School on the 1890 O.S. map, served educational purposes for a long time. From before World War I until 1977 it was Whiteley Wood (Open Air) School, then Cottage Lane School. It accommodated up to 145 boys and girls aged 5-16 and 'delicate', i.e. with physical or emotional problems or multiple handicaps. Teaching 11 subjects to CSE level, it aimed to equip them for ordinary schools. Later it was an Outdoor Education Activities Base.

The former Cottage Lane School

D Initially very narrow, the path opens into a field, to be ascended ahead to reach a ladder stile and then another close by. Follow the line indicated by the arrow on the stile post to cross the brow of the next field, from which there are distant views in many directions. At the right hand end of the line of trees, you will find a stile. Once over this, descend the very steep slope, keeping the wall about 10m to your right. A couple of marker posts should come into sight to indicate that you are on track. At the bottom you will meet a well-used path, where you should turn right.

E Continue past an open area with picnic tables and over the brook. About 5m before the second brook crossing, turn left up to a stile leading to a field. Continue up the left hand side of this field to a ladder stile and then turn half right towards a marker post. Here turn left and head for a second post about 50m away and continue ahead towards the field edge on your left.

At the end of this field, take the stile on the left into the woodland and follow the path round to the right. After about 60m, the path joins a wider one at a multi-arrowed marker post, where you should veer right and then walk parallel to the wall about 10m to your right. At the end of this wall is a marker post where you should continue ahead for about another 100m to reach a point where paths cross. An arrow on a tree indicates that you should turn right here. Follow more arrows through the wood for about 250m before reaching a stile leading into a field.

F Cross the corner of this field to another stile and then follow the path, with a wire fence on the right towards a ladder stile near buildings. Here go diagonally left across a small paddock to a stile in the far corner and then, initially keeping on about the same line, begin to cross the next field before aiming for the left hand end of the wall, where there is a stile. With a wire fence and wall on the left, then head for the gate at the main road (Hathersage Road). **See Ash House Area.**

Cross the main road and go right for a few paces before turning left into Ash House Lane and continue to the bottom (Limb Lane), where you should turn right. Walk for about 150m before crossing the road and returning to the car park.

ASH HOUSE AREA: In the 18th century the valley of the upper Ryecroft Brook was moorland, and in 1747 on ducal orders four acres were enclosed to support Dore s schoolmaster. By 1827 there were four squarish enclosures of roughly equal size on the south side of the future Ash House Lane, but the second one down now accommodated the village workhouse. Ten years later the new Ecclesall Poor Law Union made it redundant. Local schoolmaster Richard Furness lived here after his enforced resignation in 1848. A bit of wall along the Ash House drive is all that remains. The name Workhouse Lane persisted until 1950.

Whinfell Quarry Garden

Woodland path through Whirlow Brook Park

ECCLESALL WOODS AND WHIRLOW

This walk concentrates on Sheffield's largest woodland but includes an interesting section around Whirlow. Whinfell Quarry Garden is well worth the slight detour.

DISTANCE 8km (5 miles)

MINIMUM TIME 2½ hours

TERRAIN Woodland and some streets. Main roads to cross

LANDSCAPE Mainly woodland but with some open views

START/FINISH Old School, Dore

PARKING On road in Dore

PUBLIC TOILETS None on route

REFRESHMENTS Two pubs (Devonshire Arms and Hare & Hounds) and a cafe in Dore, the Rising Sun at Parkhead and Whirlow Brook Hall

TRAINS & BUSES Services 30, 98 and M17

Route Directions

A Turn right out of the Old School car park (Savage Lane) and continue down the road keeping the King Ecgbert Stone on your left. Continue round the right hand bend and as it straightens out turn left down a footpath next to house number 61. **See Cavendish Avenue & the Devonshires.**

CAVENDISH AVENUE & THE DEVONSHIRES: This area, we might say, is Dore s Cavendish Quarter. You pass Devonshire Road, then come Burlington Road, Cavendish Avenue and Victor Road. Cavendish is the ducal family name, from their place of origin in Suffolk. Conversely the Devonshire title just happened to be available in 1618 when James I made an earl of William Cavendish. Lord George Cavendish was created Earl of Burlington (oddly, a form of Bridlington) in 1831. This title is given to the first son of the Duke s heir. Victor Road was named after the 9th Duke.

At the next road (Gilleyfield Avenue), turn left and follow the road as it bends right and changes name to Burlington Road and descends. Take the second left into Ashfurlong Road then the first right down Cavendish Avenue. Take the first road on the left, Victor Road, and then turn right down Dore Road. Turn first left into Ryecroft Glen Road. **See Ecclesall Woods.**

ECCLESALL WOODS: Covering 130ha (320 acres), Ecclesall Woods resemble a scary gaping-mouthed version of Wales: think of Parkhead as the Lleyn Peninsula, Whirlow Bridge as St David s Head. As ancient woodlands they were for centuries manorial property, farm animals being pastured there. In the 16th century deer were hunted with crossbows. Besides coppicing and leaving other trees (standards) to grow tall for timber, charcoal was burned for iron smelting and whitecoal for lead. The woods were bought for the City in 1927.

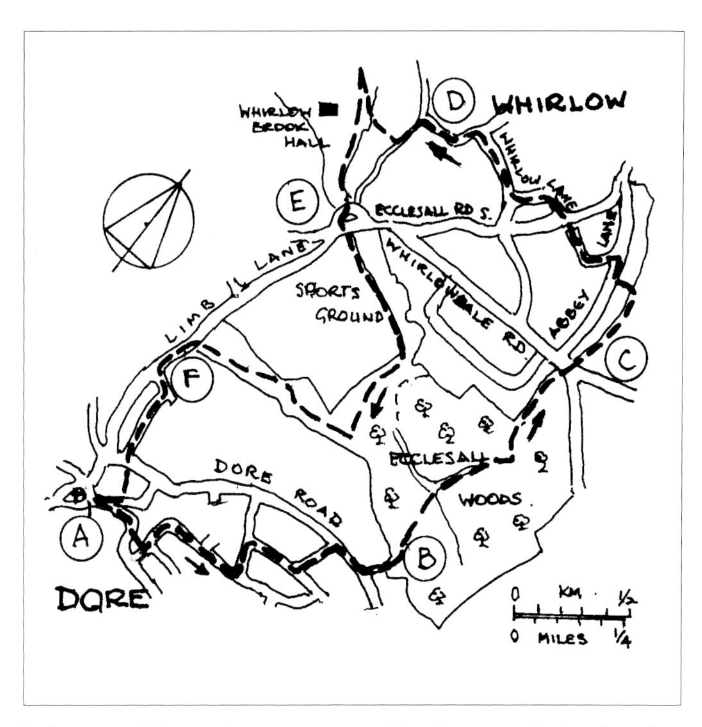

B At the bottom of the road, enter Ecclesall Woods at a public footpath sign and descend steps before crossing a small footbridge and turning left along a wide footpath, signposted to Limb Lane. In about 100m at a gate, turn right, signposted Abbeydale Road. Cross the footbridge and follow the wide path ahead uphill. At a junction of bridleways keep straight on, signposted to Abbey Lane. **See Bird Sanctuary.**

Keeping the Bird Sanctuary on your left, cross two small sleeper bridges and then, after ignoring a wide footpath on your left, proceed to a junction of paths at a bridleway sign. Turn left here and then shortly, at the next junction of paths, turn right. Cross a bridge and follow the path uphill ignoring the first signed path off to the right, signed to Abbey Lane, but taking the second, also signed to Abbey Lane.

BIRD SANCTUARY: The bird sanctuary in Ecclesall Woods was created in 1929 by Messrs A. Whitaker and C.H. Wells in cooperation with the Parks Department. At 13.5ha (33.5 acres), it comprises just over 10% of the woodland. In a survey of breeding sites 30 years ago, ornithologists found that of 25 species present the commonest was the blue tit, and other common ones were the great tit, wren, blackbird and robin. No surprises there, then, until a pair of willow tits flew in.

Almost immediately descend steps, cross a footbridge and climb up, in due course crossing over another sleeper bridge and continue to the main road junction (Abbey Lane).

C Cross straight over at this junction and re-enter the woods at a gate and continue ahead. After about 350m and at the first junction of paths, turn left and walk between laurel hedges to the main road (Abbey Lane). Turn right then shortly take the road on the left up Little Common Lane at the side of the Rising Sun public house. **See Little Common.**

LITTLE COMMON: In the 16th century Little Common was a small triangular area with the northern part of Abbey Lane at its apex and Little Common Lane at the westernmost point of the base. In her interesting book on Whirlow, Shirley Frost calls this lane its industrial area. Through the 18th century tanners were at work, with oak bark readily available from the adjacent woods. The 19th century cutlers, many of them part-time farmers, included pocket and penknife makers and scythe makers and grinders.

Climb to the end of this cul-de-sac on the left hand side and take the footpath continuing ahead. Cross the main road (Ecclesall Road South) and ascend Whirlow Lane as it winds its way up to meet a crossing road, with a sign for Whirlow Hall Farm. At this junction turn left and follow the road round a right hand bend, passing the farm buildings on your left.

D At the top of this road, where the farm buildings end, turn left onto a crossing bridleway (Coit Lane). Go through a gate and continue down. After about 200m turn right over a stile on the bank and cross the edge of the field keeping the wall on your right. Towards the end of the field and by a large tree in the wall, turn right over a stile by the wall. Cross the stile and descend through the wood into Limb Valley. At the bottom turn left along a wide path keeping Limb Brook on your right.

Coit Lane, Whirlow Hall Farm

Ignoring some smaller paths to your right, remain on the main path and follow this path to the road. This was the original Ecclesall Road South.

For a short detour to the left at this point, **see Whinfell Quarry Garden.**

WHINFELL QUARRY GARDEN: Whinfell Quarry Garden is flanked by Fenney Lane, an ancient holloway telling us how the steep part of Old Hay Lane once looked. A large house called Whinfell, burnt out in 1971 and demolished in 1979, was built around 1900 for the Doncaster family. Samuel Doncaster created the Quarry Garden with many exotic plants. The Neills took over in the 1930s, and the Garden was given to the City in 1968 after the death of Sir Frederick Neill. It is Grade II listed on the English Heritage register.

E Now turn right , passing the point where the Limb Brook goes under the road. Just before you reach the main road, cross to the left along a short paved path, leading to the main road. Cross the main road to the bus stop opposite and turn right along the footpath to Limb Lane. At the road junction double back left down another footpath signed to Ecclesall Woods. Descend along the edge of the sports field keeping the woods on your left, passing the ruins of Whirlow Wheel.

In Dore in 2008. Where?

Towards the bottom of the field the path passes between some large oak trees and descends to a stone gap stile into the woods. Follow the stone-edged path round to the right and after 100m at a signed junction of paths continue straight ahead on the stone-edged path following the sign to Abbeydale Road South. Cross several sleeper bridges and then, at a T-junction of paths at a gate, turn right onto the wide track signed to Limb Lane.

Shortly you will pass Ryecroft Glen cottage. Follow the track uphill until it passes between stone gate posts. Continue ahead for a few metres and then go through a gap in the wall on your left. Cross a stile and climb diagonally right up the field. Go straight through the car park to the road (Limb Lane).

F Cross the road, turn left and, after about 300m, turn left into Rushley Avenue and then, after about 100m, turn right down Rushley Drive and continue to the end where it meets Dore Road. Cross this road, turn left and, after about 20m, take the unsigned footpath on the right up stone steps. At the end of the footpath turn right and, with the Village Green on your left, return to the Old School.

Ecclesall Woods in autumn

OLD WOODLANDS

Covering five local woodlands, Bushey, Poynton, Old Park, Ladies Spring and Ecclesall, this walk may be better done when the trees are without leaves - if you want the views offered.

DISTANCE	8½ km (5¼ miles)
MINIMUM TIME	2½ hours
TERRAIN	Woodland paths and some pavements
LANDSCAPE	Mainly woodland
START/FINISH	Old School, Dore
PARKING	On road in Dore
PUBLIC TOILETS	None on route
REFRESHMENTS	Two pubs (Devonshire Arms and Hare & Hounds) and a cafe in Dore, Castle Inn, Abbeydale Garden Centre and Seasons cafe (Abbeydale Road South)
TRAIN & BUSES	Train and bus services 30, 97, 98, 213 and 218

Route Directions

A Leave the Old School by the large gateway and turn right (Savage Lane) to pass the Village Green on the left. Continue down and, as the road straightens out after the right hand bend, cross over and take the path to the right of house number 61.

Bushey Wood

After 75m, continue over the road and down the path ahead through narrow woodland (Bushey Wood) for about 700m, ignoring a path to the right about half way down. On reaching a road (Devonshire Road), turn right and proceed to the junction (Abbeydale Road South). **See Bradway Mill.**

BRADWAY MILL: On West View Lane you are between two mill sites, Bradway Mill to the north and Upper Wheel towards Totley. For most of their history they were jointly owned. One of them goes back at least to 1503 as a Beauchief Abbey corn mill. By the early 19th century both had become grinding wheels. Upper Wheel closed then and Bradway Mill by 1876. Its dam became successively a fishpond, a boating lake and the site of Brinkburn Drive.

B Cross the dual carriageway and continue ahead on West View Lane to ascend the flagged footpath between blocks of flats.

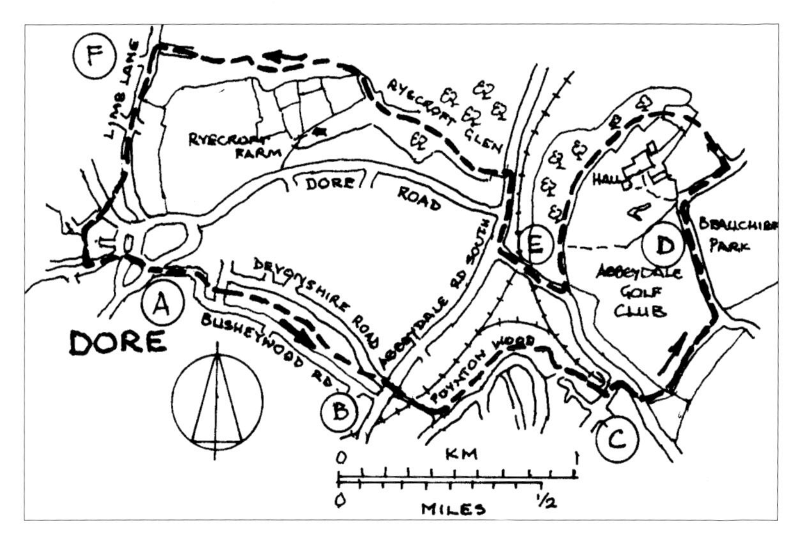

At the top and just before the steps, turn left and enter the wood (Poynton Wood). Keep straight ahead on the mainly level path ignoring all turnings off. After about 500m, the path starts to descend, with steel railings on the left, before levelling out. Continue to a junction of paths where you should turn left and follow a level path, regaining the steel railings on the left before emerging into the car park of the Castle Inn. **See Twentywell.**

TWENTYWELL: Shortly before reaching the Castle Inn, you skirt the north side of the site of Twentywell Brickworks, developed from a quarry and operating for about 75 years until closure in 1939. It was probably generated by the requirements of Bradway Tunnel, under construction 1865 -70. Brickworks and railway together prompted in 1866 the opening of the Castle Inn as a beerhouse, later extended. On emerging into Twentywell Lane you pass St Quentin s Well, now a spring in a front garden.

C Turn left along the road (Twentywell Road) to the T-junction. Here, turn right and climb the hill for 150m. Cross to the public footpath sign on the left, ascend the steps and continue ahead through woodland (Old Park Wood). The golf course soon appears to the left. Follow this path alongside the course for about 350m to reach a short flight of wooden steps. Climb the steps, turn left and walk down a wide track with the golf course now on both sides. Continue for about 500m to reach a metal gate.

About 50m before the gate, note the small stone milestone on the right.

Milestone near Beauchief Hall

D Go through the gate and continue in the same direction. The track becomes a tarmac road at the entrance to Beauchief Hall on the left. **See Beauchief & Beauchief Hall**. Turn right following the tarmac road and pass an unsigned path in a wide lay-by on the left (Gulleys Wood on the right) before reaching a path to the left.

BEAUCHIEF & BEAUCHIEF HALL: Beauchief Abbey made its mark around here St Quentin s W ell, reminiscent of St Quentin in northern France, near PrØmontrØ where the White Canons originated; Ladies Spring Wood, probably recalling the Abbey s dedication to St Mary (Our Lady) and St Thomas of Canterbury and after most of it had been dismantled the stone was re-used by Edward Pegge in 1671 to turn Beauchief Grange into Beauchief Hall. The Pegges, later Pegge-Burnells, remained its owners for over 250 years.

At this point you may wish to continue ahead for about 300m to Beauchief Abbey, with its ponds often the home of the beautifully coloured Mandarin Ducks. If you go there, retrace your steps to the signpost.

Turn left into a signed public footpath – part of the Sheffield Round Walk (SRW). Continue ahead, with a golf course on the right, to a junction of paths. Here turn half-right into woodland (Ladies Spring Wood), to follow the SRW sign.

The path swings left with rhododendrons soon marking the boundary of Beauchief Hall up to the left. Descend the steps to the Ladies Spring Wood Information Board. Here bear left and, ignoring paths to the left, continue for about 250m to reach a marker post where the path forks. Take the path on the right and continue for about 100m to reach a second post. Turn right down the steps to reach railings with a gap. Pass through, turn left and then soon reach a road (Twentywell Lane).

E Cross over before turning right downhill and then, having gone over both railway bridges, re-cross the road to go through the white gate that opens into a path leading to Dore & Totley Station. From the car park, go to the main road (Abbeydale Road South), turn right, go past the garden centre and the bottom of Dore Road and after about 100m cross the main road near the Glen Nursing Home.

Take the signed public footpath on the left and enter the woods (Ecclesall Woods). Follow the signs for Limb Lane for about 1½km (1 mile), with the Limb Brook alongside for much of the way. **See Moorbottom Farm.**

MOORBOTTOM FARM: About 100m before Limb Lane you pass on your left a wall with traces of a blocked-up window. This is all that remains of Moorbottom Farm house, home c.1850-60 of John Read, a partner in the Sheffield Smelting Company. He had rented Norton Hall and Ryecroft and bought The Moss in Limb Lane and then Derwent Hall with its huge estate. There he went bankrupt and was forced to downsize to Moorbottom. He was a trustee of Dore School for 40 years.

F On reaching the road (Limb Lane), cross over and turn left along the pavement to head towards Dore. **See Spinning Gate.**

Immediately after house number 87, turn right along a path between houses soon to meet a road (Causeway Head Road).

SPINNING GATE: There are footpath options here. The only one of historical interest goes off to your right immediately below Rushley Close. The antiquarian S.O. Addy recorded its name as Spinning Gate, evoking a folk-memory that hemp was spun here. If so, Spinning Gate could have been a rope-walk. This was a marshy area (Rushleys!) and offered the stagnant water needed for steeping the hemp stalks. The product might have been used in nearby mines or to manufacture canvas.

Turn left and, after about 80m, cross into The Meadway and continue for about 100m before taking a signed path to the left. This passes the sports ground on the right before reaching a road (Townhead Road). Turn left here and continue for about 200m to a junction with the Hare & Hounds pub ahead. Cross the road, turn left and then turn right into Savage Lane to reach the Old School after 50m.

Ecclesall Woods

MOORWOOD'S HALL AND STORTH HOUSE

This interesting walk covers an area, to the south of Dore, not often walked but providing excellent views over the village and the upper Sheaf Valley.

DISTANCE	9¼km (5¾ miles)
MINIMUM TIME	3 hours
TERRAIN	Some pavement and road but generally grass paths
LANDSCAPE	Some suburban but mainly woodland and farmland
START/FINISH	Old School, Dore
PARKING	On road in Dore
PUBLIC TOILETS	None on route
REFRESHMENTS	Two pubs (Devonshire Arms and Hare & Hounds) and a cafe in Dore, Cricket Inn, Crown Inn (just off route), Shepley Spitfire, Totley Deli cafe and Seasons cafe
TRAINS & BUSES	Bus services 30, 97, 98, 213, 218 and M17

Route Directions

A Take the small gateway out of the yard and turn right (Vicarage Lane) to pass the church. At the T-junction, turn left into Church Lane and continue until about 50m past Old Hay Close, where a signed footpath goes down to the left. Where this path opens into a field, head for the opening in the middle of the lower boundary wall.

Descend the steps and, after a short distance, cross a bridge. Turn right here at the path junction. Follow this path to the road (Old Hay Lane)). Turn left here and go for about 100m before turning right into Penny Lane.

You have just passed, on your left, the house called Totley Grove, the site of Upper Mill. **See Upper Mill.** *As you enter Penny Lane, notice the remains of a large spoil heap on your right. This was created during the building of Totley Tunnel.* **See Totley Tunnel.**

UPPER MILL: A corn mill here is mentioned first in the early 17th century and finally in 1833. The last corn miller, Joshua Hodgkinson, went over to scythe grinding here. All was over by the early 1850s. The mill workings were mostly within the perimeter of Totley Grove, whose builder and first resident, J.G. Waterfall, dismantled them. From the footpath to Hillfoot Road look to your right for a fine view of the alders flanking the brook. They gave the place its former name, Oudah.

TOTLEY TUNNEL: The Dore and Chinley Railway Act was passed in July 1884 but, through failure to raise enough capital, work began only in 1888 with powers transferred to the Midland Railway. The tunnel and track were completed by September 1893, and opened to goods traffic in November and to passengers in May 1894. The tunnel is 6.139km (3.8 miles) long. In *Totley and the Tunnel*, Brian Edwards tells lots of colourful stories about the navvies who built it.

B Immediately after the Cricket Inn, take the path diagonally across the field indicated by a sign on the left.

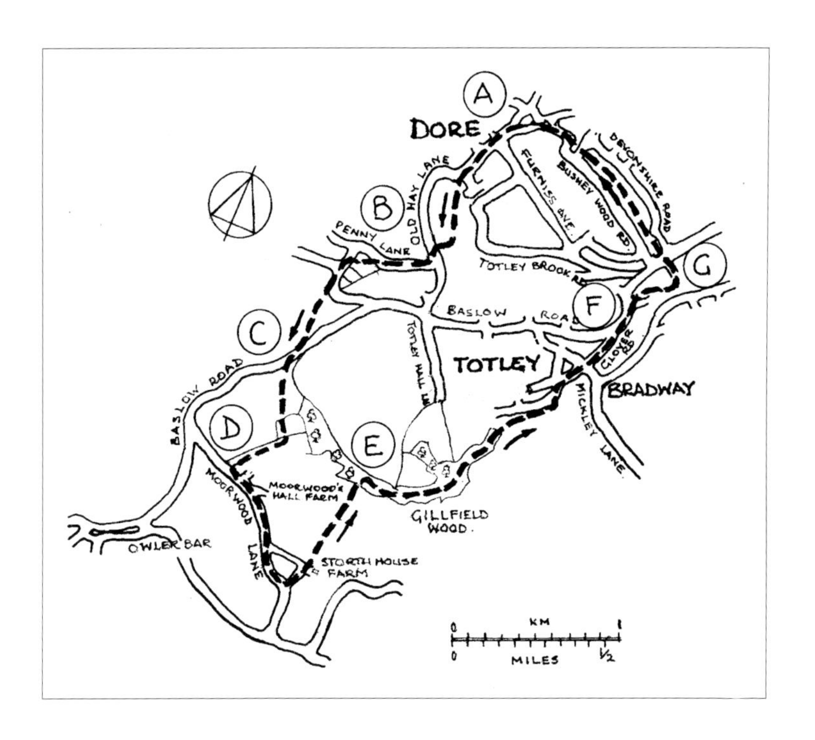

Path up to Totley from the Cricket Inn

At the end of this field, turn left and go for about 200m along the road, until a track goes right just before a bridge (over Needham's Dike). Bear right along this track and, just after a ford in the track, take the path up to the left. Turn right after the stile and follow the path as best you can through the bushes until it emerges into an open area, where ahead you will see a stile in a broken wall and wire fence. After this, bear slightly to the left and look for the next stile at the right hand end of the rails alongside the road up to your left.

Looking up the road, you will see the offices of Totley Brickworks. **See Totley Brickworks**. *Also, looking across to your right, locate a flattish area of land below the hillside. This was the location of Totley Rifle Range.* **See Totley Rifle Range.**

C At the road (Baslow Road), turn right, and after about 80m, just before the bend, cross the road and take the stile beside the footpath sign. Follow the line of this sign towards another stile over the wall. Here, take the lower (or right) of the two paths, which follows the same line as the path you have just used.

TOTLEY BRICKWORKS: Totley Brickworks (Moor Edge Silica Brickworks) was opened in 1876 by Chadwick & Barker beside an earlier brickmaking site. During the construction of Totley Tunnel the yard supplied millions of lining bricks. It had its own tramway down to No. 4 shaft, next to the area where the Rifle Range would later be built. In 1900 Pickford Holland bought the works and manufactured furnace and refractory bricks, using local ganister. In 2008 Dyson Refractories were the owners.

After about 100m, cross the wooden stile and continue to a metal gate. This next path takes you through a copse to another wooden stile, after which cross a small plank bridge and go over a wall.

TOTLEY RIFLE RANGE: According to Stephen Johnson, the Hallamshire Rifles Volunteer Corps of 1859 evolved into the 3rd Battalion, Duke of Wellington s Regiment (West Riding) Yorkshire Volunteers of 1992. Having adopted the .303 rifle it had to move out of town for safety reasons. The Totley site was leased from the Duke of Rutland in 1900 and bought in 1920. The range was constructed and opened in 1900 and remodelled in the late 1970s. The Sheffield Association of Shooting Clubs uses it too.

Keeping the wall on your right, continue to a further stile in the field corner. Here turn right and, keeping the wall on your right, pass through three five-bar gates until you reach a field with a metal gate ahead.

D Go through this unusual gate (*you'll see why*), turn left along the road (Moorwood Lane) to pass Moorwood's Hall Farm and a lodge on the left. About 300m past the lodge, turn left into a drive signed public footpath that leads to Storth Farm.

Calling Bell, Storth House

To the left of the buildings, find a squeeze stile into a small enclosure. Cross this to take the stile ahead and then head downhill, aiming just to the right of two white gas pipeline markers. Continue to the gate ahead and then bear slightly left to follow the foundations of an old wall to the next stile. Having crossed this, bear right towards an open gateway and then, bearing away from the fence/wall on your right, head towards a stile in the lower boundary wall.

E Cross this and, after a short rise within the wood (Gillfield Wood), turn right on to a wide track. **See Gillfield Wood.**

GILLFIELD WOOD: The City of Sheffield owns and maintains Gillfield Wood, in effect a plantation of larch, sycamore and American red oak. Back in 1561 it was a coppice wood. Melvin Jones explains the 4-5m wide depressions, often down steep slopes, as kilns for producing whitecoal. This was a special wood fuel used to smelt lead by means of water-powered bellows, a process introduced c1575 and replaced by 1750 by coal-fired cupolas.

Follow this track through the wood, keeping the brook (Totley Brook) on your right, until you reach a more open area with houses to your left. The path soon runs beside the gardens of the houses before coming to a tarmac area with the Totley Scouts HQ ahead. Turn left here between houses to reach a road (Aldam Road), where you should turn right and head towards crossroads. Turn right into Green Oak Road to come to another crossroad junction and there take Glover Road ahead.

F At the end of Glover Road, continue ahead with the shops on your right and then pass the end of Milldale Road. 50m further on, fork right into Mill Lane, which soon narrows to a footpath to cross a brook into a wood. **See Totley Rolling Mill**.

TOTLEY ROLLING MILL: Mill Lane went to yet another lead smelting mill, first mentioned in 1612, run by Thomas Hall and Leonard Gill and later known as Hall s House. It passed through the hands of many owners notably the Burtons of Holmesfield and occupiers. In the 18th century they added a cutlers grinding wheel, cupola and lead rolling mill, used from c1840 for rolling steel. The dam, like a misshapen parsnip, lay beneath Milldale Road and behind the Totley Rise shops

The path ahead climbs until it meets a paved path with a handrail, where you should turn left downhill. At the bottom, continue ahead into West View Lane to cross the railway and river before reaching the dual carriageway (Abbeydale Road South). Cross and take Devonshire Road to the right of the Tesco Express.

G Keeping on the left hand side of this road, look for a public footpath after 100m. This path, initially with a small stream on the left, goes the full length of Bushey Wood (ignore a branch off to the left after about 300m) before coming to a road (Gilleyfield Avenue). **See Bushey Wood.** Cross and continue directly ahead on the footpath for about 60m before coming to another road (Savage Lane) where you should bear right uphill. The village green and the Old School soon come into view.

BUSHEY WOOD: Thought by some to be Dore s best-kept secret, this little wood was called Teppiland Bushes in the mid-17th century, after the fields to the south-west, and by its present name a century later. The Sampson family became its owners and in May 1930 Edward Sampson, surveyor to the then Norton Rural District Council, presented it to the RDC as a New Park for Dore . With the boundary change of 1935 it passed to Sheffield City Council.

The Cricket Inn, Penny Lane

Old Hay Brook in autumn

DORE MILL TRAIL

Every stream and river in Sheffield was harnessed to provide power for the city's industry. This walk traces the streams in the Dore area and the dams and mills that used to draw on them.

DISTANCE	9½km (6 miles)
MINIMUM TIME	3 hours
TERRAIN	Fields, woodland and suburban footpaths
LANDSCAPE	Suburban, countryside and views
START/FINISH	Old School, Dore
PARKING	On road in Dore
PUBLIC TOILETS	None on route
REFRESHMENTS	Two pubs (Devonshire Arms and Hare & Hounds) and a cafe in Dore, Seasons cafe (on Abbeydale Road South) and Abbeydale Garden Centre. Cricket Inn and Crown pubs slightly off route
TRAINS & BUSES	Train and bus services 30, 97, 98, 213, 218 and M17

Route Directions

A Leave the Old School by the large gateway, turn left (Savage Lane), cross the road ahead (High Street) and turn right up Townhead Road. Keep on past the entrance to the recreation ground and Cromwell Cottage, built in 1686 and 400 years after the earliest recorded water mill in the area. At Knowle Green the wide verge on your right is all that remains of one of the village's ancient greens. Go ahead down Whitelow Lane. **See Wag Wood.**

B Crossing the brook (Redcar Brook), the lane passes the steps to Wagg Cottage on the right. Turn left into Shorts Lane. After 90m cross a stile on the left to follow the line of the field footpath sign to the right across two uneven fields until it joins the stream bank at a stile through a hawthorn hedge. Immediately cross a second stile and follow the stream to a further stile, where looking back to the stream you will see a weir. It was from here that water from the brook was directed under the field to our next mill site.

In case you are wondering, the correct spelling appears to be Wag, even though the cottage name has the double 'g'.

WAG WOOD: Wag Wood on the right by the brook is shown as Cupola Bank on old maps and no doubt a track led through the field gate on the right to the Upper Smelting Mill. Looking upstream from the modern bridge, the Mill was sited on the right bank of Redcar Brook opposite Wagg Cottage, which can be seen across a field on the right of the road and to the left of the river. The lost site of Cliff Smelting Mill must have been further upstream in the woods.

Cross the stile and a bridge, then a further two stiles to the access drive to Avenue Farm. Turn right, crossing back over the stream (Redcar Brook)

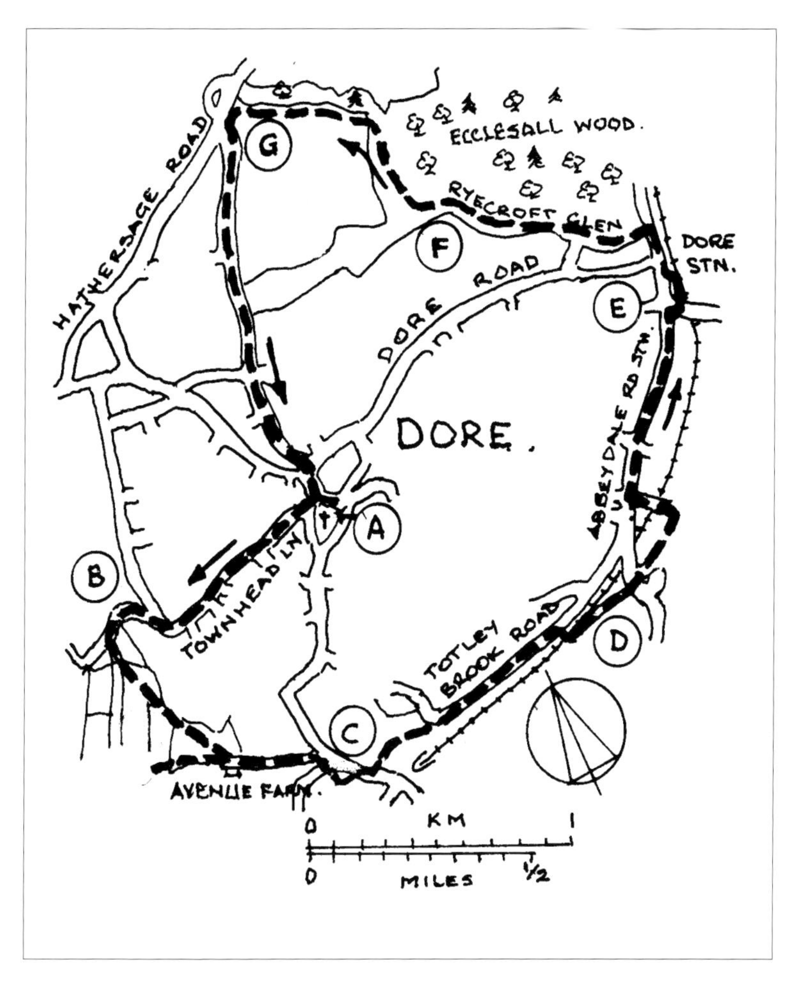

and passing around a gate, before continuing ahead up the field to join a new stream (Blacka Dyke) on the left. This contains a small weir directing water towards a dam on its opposite side. **See Totley Forge**.

After visiting the breached dam some 40m upstream, retrace your steps downstream through the gate and past Avenue Farm, built in 1891 by the famous Sheffield industrialist Joshua Tyzack.

TOTLEY FORGE: This was one of two dams that held water for Totley Forge, the buildings of which are hidden from view behind Avenue Farm. Slightly further upstream is the silted up remains of an upper dam breached, but still with its stone overflow shuttle. In the bank almost under your feet is the outflow from a pipe that also brought water from above the first crossing point on Redcar Brook. The two dams powered a paper mill before 1653 and later a scythe forge.

Continue along this metalled track to meet a road (Old Hay Lane).

Immediately before the road, turn right at a public footpath sign through a gate between stone pillars onto a path that goes down flagstone steps and over a footbridge to a metalled drive. Turn right up this drive past two houses to a partly overgrown field gate on your right. **See Oldhay Lead Mill.**

OLDHAY LEAD MILL: The area behind this was the dam for Oldhay Lead Mill, recorded in 1585 and later converted to grinding scythes early last century, now subsumed into the modern house, Fall Cottage, below it. The works closed in 1895, the grinding shop was demolished in 1909 and in 1933 the dam was filled in. Historically this is amongst the most important sites in the area, being one of the earliest to have a water-powered ore-hearth smelt mill and certainly the first reverberatory or cupola furnace in Derbyshire and perhaps in the country.

C Retrace your steps down the drive past the large house on your left, Old Hay, which was converted from the managers' cottages contemporary with the mill. At the bottom of the drive turn right onto the lane for about 150m, then left over a stile onto a path with a high wall on your right behind which are the grounds of Totley Grove. Shortly pass through a kissing gate onto a raised path over a stream. **See Upper Mill.**

UPPER MILL: This stream is the outflow of a dam on Needham s Dike that fed a corn mill sited by the side of the Grove as early as 1625. Latterly used for scythe grinding, the mill was demolished about 1852 at the time Totley Grove was built, but some of the mill outbuildings still stand to the rear of the house.

Continue on the right bank of the stream (Oldhay Brook). Just before you cross the stream on a modern bridge is another weir on your left and, just over the bridge, a Victorian holding tank on your left before you join a road (Totley Brook Road). Turn right. **See Nether Mill.**

NETHER MILL: Before the building of the Manchester railway line and the Victorian houses, a goit (man made water course) fed water from the Totley Brook behind the houses on the far side of the road to a long lost lead mill, Nether Mill, first mentioned in a 1676 will. It was later used to grind scythes and sickles.

Continue down the right side of the road and then take the path on the right over the railway to reach a road (Grove Road). Turn left, passing modern houses until Victorian ones appear on your right. You are now standing on what would have been the end of Totley Brook Road had the estate not been split by the arrival of the railway.

Oldhay Brook, with mineral staining

D Cross the main road carefully into Mill Lane, with Oldhay Brook now on your left. Walk down the lane with newly laid out gardens on your right, where sampling showed excessive levels of lead in the soil, requiring its removal and the reinstatement of the gardens. On your right is an old stone built cottage. **See Totley Rolling Mill.**

TOTLEY ROLLING MILL: This was the manager's house for Totley Rolling Mill, the dam for which occupied the valley bottom behind the shops on Totley Rise and now the site of a new housing estate. The dam site dates back to 1615, having at times been a lead mill, grinding mill and steel mill before closing in the 1880s.

The Manager's House, Totley Rolling Mill

Cross a bridge over a brook (Totley Brook) that flows under your feet to join Oldhay Brook on your left to form the River Sheaf. Continue straight on through a wooded area, bearing left after the trees on the left open out, to pass between the blocks of flats and then turn left onto a raised roadway crossing the railway. **See Upper Wheel and Bradway Mill.**

Continue to the main road, turn right passing a cul-de-sac and the Royal Artillery War Memorial Houses, either side of Brinkburn Road, on your right. The houses here are on the site of Bradway Mill.

UPPER WHEEL AND BRADWAY MILL: West View flats were built on the site of Upper Wheel of which nothing remains except traces of a head goit by the river above the flats and another leading to a lower dam and wheel, visible as a channel between the river and the railway below the road on its right hand side. This lower site was that of Bradway Mill. Both were corn mills for centuries and one had belonged to Beauchief Abbey. They ended life as grinding wheels.

Continue past Five Trees Drive and Abbeydale Hall on the other side of the main road. Pass the Post Office sorting office, once the Church Rooms. Note the mosaic commemorating its use as a First World War hospital, and turn right up Twentywell Lane. On your right, after the river and before the railway bridge, is a block of flats. **See Walk Mill.**

WALK MILL: When the Midland railway opened in 1870 it obliterated the site of the Walk Mill, the dam for which was behind and to the left of the flats. It was erected by the Canons of Beauchief Abbey, about 1280, for fulling cloth and then used as a corn mill until after the dissolution of the Abbey, when part became a cutlers wheel. In use until 1864 variously for straw-knife and sickle grinding, as a paper mill and for saw making, it was finally demolished in 1890.

E Cross the road and pass through a gate just before the railway bridge to join what was once the bottom part of Twentywell Lane. After crossing the river, pass the old Dore & Totley Station building, and then the front of the garden centre before reaching an old Victorian house on the main road on your right, the original station master's house. Here cross the main road to a narrow walled path running on the left bank of a brook (Limb

Brook), the old Derbyshire/Yorkshire boundary. This is also signed as part of the Sheffield Round Walk.

Walk upstream through woodland for about 800m, passing firstly through a gate and then in turn footpath signs to Ryecroft Glen on your left and Abbeydale Road on your right. The path passes over several bridges and another footpath sign on the right to Abbeydale Road. After crossing an old stone bridge you eventually reach a horse barrier where there is a footpath sign on the right to Whirlow. Continue upstream bearing slightly left until the ruins of a derelict building can be seen on the right. **See Ryecroft Mill.**

RYECROFT MILL: This was a lead mill in 1671 and the names of neighbouring fields, Upper Belland and Lower Belland, relate to pollution caused by the smelting. By 1800 it had become a corn wheel, with John Unwin as tenant at a rent of £12, and by 1871 it had ceased operating. Ryecroft Mill was fed by goits from both Limb Brook and Ryecroft Brook, which brook can still be traced. The dam is now largely drained, but the back of the wheel-pit can clearly be seen, with outlines of the mill building to the east.

Derelict Wheel Pit, Ryecroft Mill

F Retrace your steps to the horse gate, then turn left continuing for 300m along an old trackway. Immediately after crossing the third wooden bridge there is a footpath sign showing Abbey Lane and Whirlow. At this fork in the path, bear left up to a wall, passing through into playing fields. Continue up along the edge of the woods until a ruined building comes in view near the top of the field. **See Whirlow Wheel.** To really appreciate the site it is worth descending with care to the right of the building where the remains of the turbine are still visible at the bottom of the impressive wheel pit, which probably originally housed an overshot wheel.

WHIRLOW WHEEL: This is the remains of Whirlow Wheel. It was served by two dams, the upper one still visible in Whirlow Gardens, and the lower dam obliterated by construction of the modern road. Records of a wheel on 'Lymbrooke' go back to 1586 when it was owned by John Bright and it is probably the same corn mill listed in 1655. From 1726 to 1935 the property was administered by the Trustees of Hollis Hospital, probably working latterly as a saw and scythe grinding wheel. In 1853 William Furness took over at a rent of £30, but operation was unsatisfactory through a shortage of water allegedly due to the effect of mining. In 1901 a water turbine was installed, but by 1933 the building was dilapidated and in 1935 it was sold with the surrounding ground to the corporation. It was partly used as a Corporation store, before collapsing due to neglect in 2006.

One cannot leave this site without feeling sad that so little remains of a once busy industrial site utilising a truly renewable energy source. It would be nice to think that somewhere the funds could be found to return it to use as living proof of the power and beauty of the water wheel in its heyday.

G To return to Dore, bear left to the main road and then turn left to join Limb Lane and follow it back into the centre of the village.

GILLFIELD WOOD AND TOTLEY BENTS

Gillfield Wood, especially with its bluebells in spring, is a delightful place for a quiet stroll. This walk also explores a bit of the often-missed older part of Totley.

DISTANCE	10km (6 miles)
MINIMUM TIME	3 hours
TERRAIN	Woodland and field paths, some road walking
LANDSCAPE	Good views over Dore and Blacka from Totley
START/FINISH	Old School, Dore
PARKING	On road in Dore
PUBLIC TOILETS	None on route
REFRESHMENTS	Two pubs (Devonshire Arms and Hare & Hounds) and a cafe in Dore, Seasons cafe on Abbeydale Road South, Cross Scythes and Fleur de Lys in Totley Also Cricket Inn and Crown Inn (slightly off route)
TRAINS & BUSES	Services 30, 97, 98, 213, 218 and M17

Route Directions

A Leave the Old School yard by the large gateway and turn right (Savage Lane). Continue downhill past the Village Green on your left, following the road to a right hand bend. As the road straightens out, cross and go down the footpath to the right of number 61. At the end of the footpath, cross the road (Gilleyfield Avenue) and continue ahead down the signed footpath, with a wooden fence on the right. Continue gently downhill for about 600m, ignoring a path that goes off to your right, eventually to emerge on to a road (Devonshire Road). Turn right downhill to pass the Tesco Express on your right and reach the main road (Abbeydale Road South).

B Turn right here then cross the bottom of Bushey Wood Road and continue ahead along Totley Brook Road for about 450m. **See Dore & Totley URC.** Turn left over the railway footbridge with the Totley Tunnel East signal box down on the right. Continue ahead over a road (Grove Road) to a tarmac path between bungalows which shortly bears right with Oldhay Brook on its left. Cross the bridge on the left at a weir and climb the path through woodland (Akley Bank) to a road (The Quadrant).

DORE & TOTLEY URC: The story of Dore & Totley United Reformed Church dates from 1888. Six Congregationalists and others began worshipping in the almshouse premises opposite Dore & Totley Station. In 1889 they erected a second-hand iron church across the road. This tin tabernacle was their place of worship for 25 years, seeing removal to Totley Brook Road in 1908. The Union Church was built in 1913, and the tin tab became the church hall for another 16 years. As we went to press the church was once more undergoing renewal.

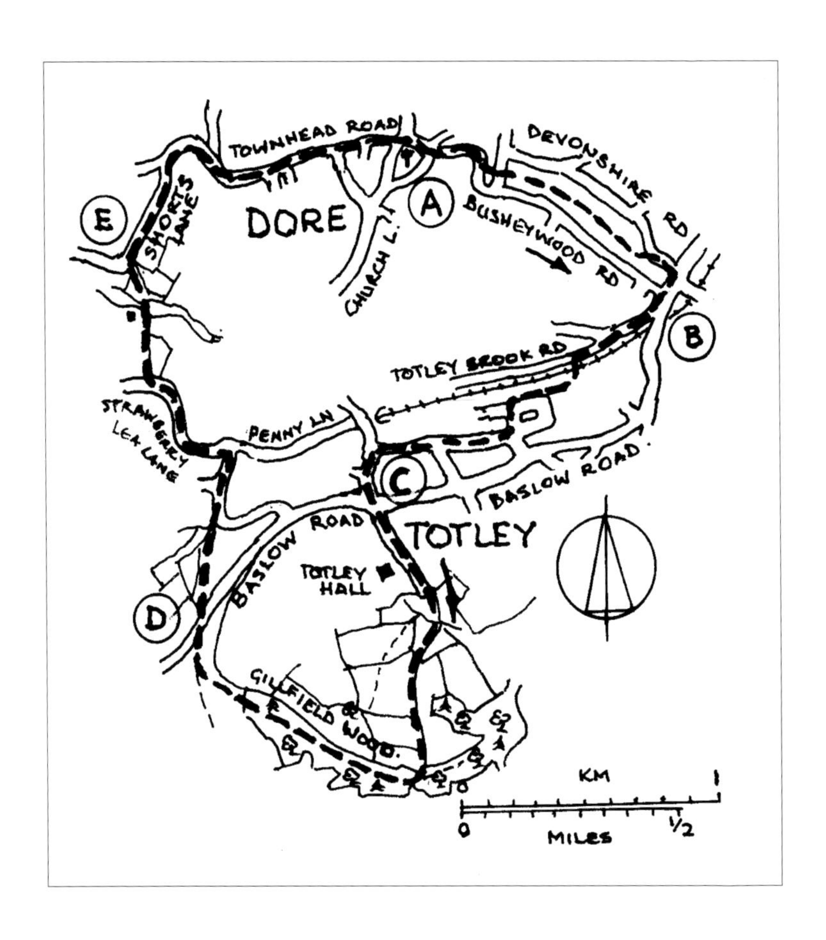

Turn right here and then, after about 50m, turn left into Terrey Road. After a further 100m, turn right up The Grove and continue for about 500m to the end of the cul-de-sac. Here take the left path of three for 50m to reach a road (Butts Hill). **See Butts Hill & Cannon Hall.**

At this point, it is worth taking a short detour to the left to see a group of Totley's older houses, including Cannon Hall. Retrace your steps afterwards.

Turn right and, after about 50m, turn left (Hillfoot Road), up to Baslow Road.

BUTTS HILL & CANNON HALL: Unless from a surname, Butts Hill evokes compulsory Sunday archery practice for able-bodied males, supervised by the parish constable, under laws of around 1500. Cannon Hall perhaps takes its name from the White Canons of Beauchief who came this way to their grange at Strawberry Lee. Grade II listed, it incorporates a cruck building with two remaining sets of crucks, probably late medieval. The length of the crucks makes it unusually high. The western section has been altered and an extension added.

C Using the pedestrian crossing, cross into Totley Hall Lane and continue for about 500m to the gate at the end. Here cross the stile and take the middle track of three, bearing slightly to the right. Cross another stile keeping on the same track and then, after about 200m, turn left into a field.

Fleur de Lys, Totley

With a hedge on your right, go for another 200m to reach a gate into woodland (Gillfield Wood). Enter the wood and almost immediately turn right and follow the way-marked path for about 700m.

In May, this stretch of the walk has extensive areas of bluebells on both sides.

Gillfield Wood

Cross a stile and keep straight on, skirting the edge of new woodland created by the Forestry Commission. Where the path meets a track, continue ahead to a stone stile and cross an area covered with crushed road material to reach another stile at the main road (Baslow Road).

D Cross the road, turn right and continue for about 100m before turning left at a footpath sign. Follow the path diagonally right down the field to a double stile. Continue down, crossing two small wooden bridges and a stile. Turn right at the lane, cross a ford (containing Needham's Dike) and continue ahead to reach a road (Lane Head Road). Turn left, pass Moss Road and continue for about 250m to a road junction (Totley Bents) with a large house, The Grouse, ahead and Penny Lane on your right.

At this point, you may wish to divert to the Cricket Inn, across the sports field, for refreshment.

Turn left up Strawberry Lee Lane and follow it for about 500m and, shortly after the road bears to the left, turn right at the footpath sign. Descend the path, cross a footbridge and continue ahead between walls. Go through a gap stile, cross another bridge and ascend the field ahead with the fence on your right.

E Turn right along the lane (Shorts Lane) and at the end turn right and follow this road (Whitelow Lane becoming Townhead Road) for about 1km back to the village centre. With the Hare & Hounds immediately ahead of you, cross the road, turn left and then turn right down Savage Lane for about 50m to reach the Old School.

SHEAF VALLEY HEAD

The elevated route of this walk round the head of the Sheaf Valley provides ever-changing views of the Dore, Totley and Bradway areas. Take your binoculars for extra interest.

DISTANCE	10¾km (6¾ miles)
MINIMUM TIME	3½ hours
TERRAIN	Pavement, bridleways, quiet rural lanes and field paths
LANDSCAPE	Farm and moorland, with some urban sections
START/FINISH	Old School, Dore
PARKING	On road in Dore
PUBLIC TOILETS	None on route
REFRESHMENTS	Two pubs (Devonshire Arms and Hare & Hounds) and a cafe in Dore, Seasons cafe on Abbeydale Road South, deli cafe at Totley Rise and Shepley Spitfire pub
TRAINS & BUSES	Bus services 30, 97, 98, 213, 218 and M17

Route Directions

A Leave the Old School yard by the large gateway and turn right (Savage Lane). Continue downhill past the Village Green on your left, following the road to a right hand bend. As the road straightens out, cross over and go down the footpath to the right of number 61.

Footbridge, Bushey Wood

At the end of the footpath, cross the road (Gilleyfield Avenue) and continue ahead down the signed footpath, with a wooden fence on the right. Continue gently downhill for about 600m, ignoring a path that goes off to your right, eventually to emerge on to a road (Devonshire Road). Turn right downhill to pass the Tesco Express on your right and reach the main road (Abbeydale Road South).

B Go straight ahead across the main road into West View Lane, crossing the river and railway. Immediately past the first block of flats, turn right and go via Kalman Walk into a small wood after the flats. Bear left slightly uphill to join a larger path close to a wooden footbridge. Turn right onto this path, shortly crossing another footbridge to reach a surfaced path, which becomes a small road by Mill House. This reaches the footpath alongside the dual carriageway (Abbeydale Road South). Turn left, pass Milldale Road and, after a further 20m, turn left just before the parade of

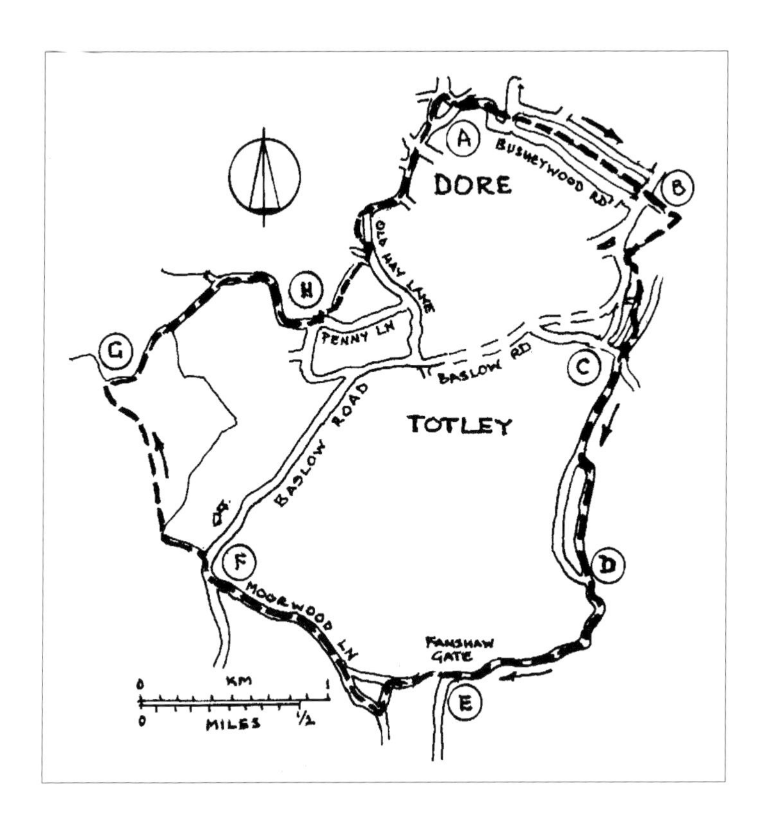

shops. Follow the narrow lane between houses and continue ahead where this joins a service road, with a brook on your left.After a short distance, take a footpath on your left that crosses the brook, bearing right to walk up a drive (Back Lane). When you reach the road, turn right and, at the next road (Mickley Lane), go straight across to the Shepley Spitfire.

C Take the signed public bridleway to the left of the pub, going gently uphill initially. Continue for 450m, passing a phone mast in a field on your left, dipping slightly to cross a stream via a bridge. This is the county boundary. After the stream, bear left up hill and, after a short distance as the main (private) track turns to the right, turn left off this main track. At this point there are two options. The first left turn is a sunken track between old hedges. If this is muddy, take the second left turn which is a path that runs at a higher level than but parallel to the sunken track. Both paths arrive at a tarmac lane at farm buildings.

D Continue straight ahead on the lane, passing between farm buildings and then Woodthorpe Hall on your right. Go along the winding Fanshaw Gate Lane for about 1.4km (almost 1 mile), eventually passing Fanshawe Gate Old Hall on the right, with its small knot garden on the gravelled forecourt, then Fanshawe Gate House and the caravan site entrance. At the top of the hill, where the road bends sharply left, go right over a stile or through a metal gate to join a footpath.

E The footpath goes downhill into trees, initially with a low wall on your right, eventually picking up a wire fence on the right. Turn right over a stile adjacent to a large pond and walk with the pond on your left to reach a stile on the right of a gate by farm buildings. Continue ahead on a grassy track which bears right in due course to reach a junction with the farm drive.

Turn left here and then walk up the drive to meet a road (Moorwood Lane). Turn right and continue for about 1200m (almost ¾ mile), passing unusual gritstone gateposts on the right, to meet the main road (A 621).

Gateposts, Moorwood's Farm

F Turn right downhill for a short distance, passing Moor Edge Farm entrance on your right. About 60m beyond this entrance cross the road, taking great care as the view is poor from the inside of the bend, to take a concessionary bridleway going left uphill from the road. Pass through a gate and follow the path bending right to pick up a wall on your right, and meet a broader track where the wall bends to the right.

Turn right on this track along the hillside. **See Duke's Drive.** After about 700m the path begins to rise, bending left then right to cross a small stream with a low retaining wall, just visible on the right. Just after the stream, take a narrower path off to the right that goes slightly downhill to meet a broad, rutted track, with a wall beyond, near a gate.

DUKE S DRIVE: The Duke s Drive, one of several such, was designed by Charles Cecil John, 6th Duke of Rutland (1815-88), known as the Sporting Duke. They were intended to give access to the grouse moors of his Longshaw estate and were laid out between 1857, as soon as he succeeded to the dukedom, and 1870.

G Turn right though the gate and continue downhill on an increasingly rocky track to cross a road where on your left is a gateway and an unsigned drive to Bolehill Lodge. **See Bole Hill.**

BOLE HILL: This indicates an early lead-smelting site. The bole was a small low-walled area on a hillside exposed to the prevailing south-westerlies. A wood or peat fire was kindled and covered alternately with ore and more fuel. The draught entered through holes in the wall and the lead flowed through another into a pool outside. After 1565 mills with water-powered bellows took over.

Continue straight ahead on the rocky track, signposted as a public byway, that goes downhill to meet another track. Turn right onto what soon becomes a surfaced lane (Strawberry Lee Lane) and continue along the lane, ignoring any side lanes or paths.

The Grouse, Totley Bents

Shortly after the brow of the hill, the lane bears left, and on the right, opposite the first roadside buildings you encounter, is one of the spoil heaps and ventilation shafts from the Totley Tunnel construction. Shortly you reach a junction with Lane Head Road on the right and Penny Lane straight ahead. **See Totley Bents.**

TOTLEY BENTS: Bents means a place covered in rushes or reedy grass. Totley Bents s liveliest historical feature was the Grouse Inn in its heyday. Dr Keith Blackburn told us years ago that the building thus called was erected by a farmer, Clement Needham, as a doss-house for the railway navvies of 1889-93. The pub was at the back, originally a beerhouse opened in the 1830s. It closed in 1956. The Cricket Inn may have begun as a beerhouse in the early 1860s. Lower Bents, opposite, figures in a deed of 1621.

H Go ahead about 20m down Penny Lane, turn left along a surfaced track, a signed public footpath with stables on the left, for 50 metres. Then turn right downhill on a grassy track with a wall on your right to reach a stone stile.

Cross the stile and immediately turn left to follow a fence/hedge on your left. The path arrives at a house with a flagstone roof. Cross a stone stile adjacent to the house wall, pass between the house and garage and continue down the lane as it bends to the right. Immediately after masonry gateposts at the house named Old Hay, turn left onto a path to cross a footbridge and climb steps to the road.

Go ahead, not left to Avenue Farm, to a stile between stone posts and then take the signed path up the field with a wall on your right. Leave the field at the top right hand corner over a high stone step stile and continue ahead on the road (Old Hay Lane), which becomes Church Lane, to the village centre. Continue ahead past the church and the Hare & Hounds pub, then turn right down Savage Lane, to reach the Old School on the right.

Old Hay Lane, leading to Hillfoot Road

THE COFFIN ROUTES

These two routes, from Dore to Dronfield, were probably used to take the dead for burial before Dore had its own churchyard. They make a rewarding change from typical Peak District walks.

DISTANCE	12¾km (8 miles), 10¼km (6¼m) if short cut taken
MINIMUM TIME	4 hours
TERRAIN	Grass paths, tracks and some suburban pavements
LANDSCAPE	Suburban, farmland and a golf course
START/FINISH	Old School, Dore
PARKING	On road in Dore
PUBLIC TOILETS	Dronfield Sports Centre
REFRESHMENTS	Two pubs (Devonshire Arms and Hare & Hounds) and a cafe in Dore. Seasons cafe on Abbeydale Road South, deli and coffee shop at Bradway. In Dronfield, Coffee Central on High Street and deli on Stubley Lane
TRAINS & BUSES	Bus services 30, 97, 98, 213, 218, 293 and M17

Route Directions

This walk is an 'out and return' trip to Dronfield totalling 12¾km (8 miles), but it can be reduced to 10¼km (6½ miles) by avoiding Dronfield centre.

COFFIN ROUTES (aka CORPSE ROADS): Dore and Totley people could not be buried at Dore until November 1829 when a graveyard, later extended, was opened west of the new chapel-of-ease. Up to then the dead had to be carried to the mother church at Dronfield (and occasionally still were). The main route is likely to have been via Bushey Wood, continuing as a corpse road through Upper Bradway. A possible secondary route via Water Lane would have been slightly longer but avoided the fearsome ascent up the bank almost opposite the present Devonshire Road.

A Leave the Old School by the large gateway, turn right (Savage Lane) and continue down with the Village Green on the left. After 250m, where the road straightens out after the right hand bend, take the unsigned footpath on the left, just after house number 61, to reach a road (Gilleyfield Avenue). Cross and continue ahead on the signed path for about 700m through a narrow strip of woodland (Bushey Wood), ignoring a branch path to the right half way down. When the path reaches a road (Devonshire Road), turn right and continue for 100m to Abbeydale Road South.

Cross this road, enter West View Lane and continue over the river and railway to reach a railed path ahead. Go up here, then up the steps at the top to reach a road (Prospect Place) and continue uphill to the left for about 80m to reach another road (Prospect Road). **See Upper Bradway & Tinker's Corner.** Turn left here and, ignoring all roads to the left, walk for

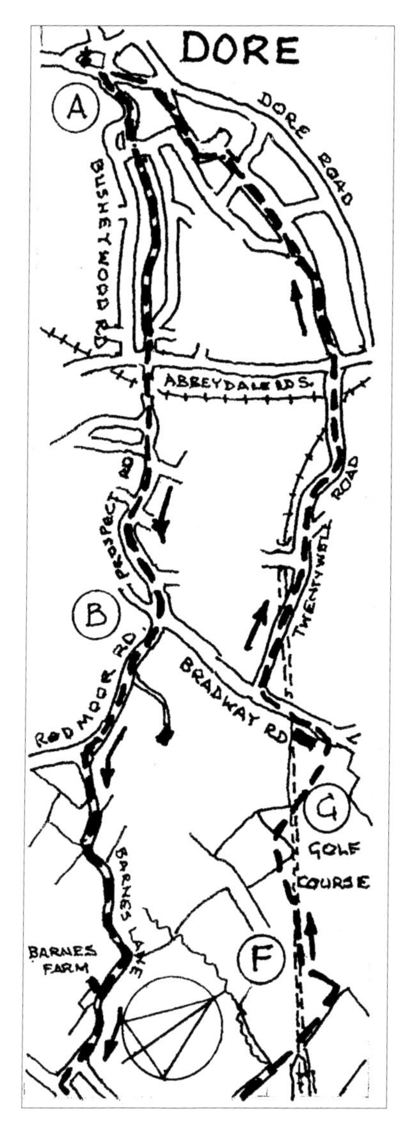

about 700m to reach a staggered crossroads.

B Go straight ahead into the signed Bradway Road. At the Derbyshire boundary and road speed derestriction signs, cross the road and continue on the pavement to reach a steeper section of road with a right hand curve.

On the crown of the bend cross the road with care and enter a lane on the left leading to Birchitt Farm. After about 50m, where the lane forks, take the right fork on a signed footpath (Barnes Lane). Continue on this old lane for about 1km, ignoring a path to the left where the lane bends to the right, eventually reaching a farm on the right. Here the path becomes first a roughly paved road and then a normal road that continues ahead to reach houses, shops and a main road (Stubley Lane/Carr Lane).

UPPER BRADWAY & TINKER S CORNER:
Roughly at the junction of Prospect Road and Rosamond Drive you regained the coffin route that you left at Abbeydale Road South. As Tony Smith, Bradway s historian, has shown, this joined another corpse road from Totley at Tinker s Corner, the staggered crossroads: here on your right is Totley Lane, the modern end of an ancient bridleway from the foot of Mickley Lane. Tinker s Corner is named after local entrepreneur Tedbar Tinker (Twentywell Quarry and Brickworks, Totley Chemical Yard). He lived at The Grange, in the south-east angle.

Turn left here and continue for about 500m, passing a service station on the right, to a road junction where Stubley Lane turns to the right (with the road ahead changing into Stubley Hollow).

If you wish to shorten the walk, continue ahead into Stubley Hollow and descend for about 250m until you are opposite Summerwood Lane. Rejoin the walk at letter E by taking the stile on the left.

C Bear right to continue on Stubley Lane which, after passing over a dual carriageway, reaches roundabouts after about 750m where you should take the third exit (Wreakes Lane becoming High Street) leading to the Civic Centre. Continue down past the cross on the right into Church Street and then round the bends soon to reach the Parish Church of St John the Baptist. **See Dronfield Church.**

You may wish to have a look at both the church and the churchyard, with its headstones of former Dore residents.

DRONFIELD CHURCH: The remains of a preaching cross add weight to the theory of pre-Domesday Christian activity here. St John the Baptist s Church existed at least by 1135. It was also Dore s parish church until 1843, although by the 17th century a chapel-of-ease at Dore made attending worship and baptisms a lot easier. Dronfield s nave is the oldest part of the church, followed about 1200 by the south aisle and a century later by the huge chancel. In 1392 Ralph Barker of Dore and others endowed an existing chantry (to pay priests to sing masses) and in 1399 he gave Beauchief Abbey his right to nominate priests to the benefice.

A Dore grave, Dronfield churchyard

D Leave the church grounds by the lych gate (Church Street), turn right and retrace your steps to continue uphill to enter High Street. Then pass the cross to reach the roundabouts close to the Sainsbury's store and take Stubley Lane which, after 300m, passes over the dual carriageway.

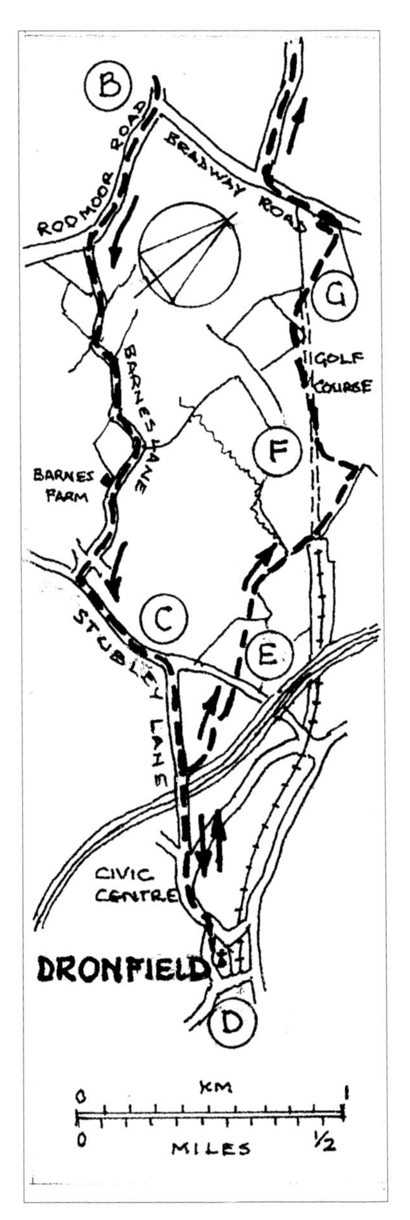

Immediately after this bridge, take the signed path on the right. Initially with a fence on the right, it soon passes between houses and continues ahead into an unmade road (Summerwood Lane). Ignore the path to the left but continue down to reach a road (Stubley Hollow).

E Cross the road and take the footpath directly opposite leading into a field. The path continues ahead over the field with a wall on the left and then crosses over a stile with a dressage ring on the left. Continue ahead over another stile and then bear diagonally right over the brow of the field and then head for a metal gate in the far corner.

Take the stile on the right of the large tree and then down the next field, keeping the hedge on the left. Take the wooden footbridge over the stream and continue ahead, now with a wire fence on the right. Shortly cross the stile ahead next to the metal fence which encloses the southern end of the Bradway Tunnel, and continue on the path between small trees soon to see a golf course on the left. **See Bradway Tunnel.**

BRADWAY TUNNEL: For 30 years after 1840, Sheffield people wanting to travel south by train had to take roundabout routes: initially north-east via Rotherham, then east via Eckington. In 1864 the Midland Railway Co. s Sheffield-Chesterfield line was authorized. The Bradway Tunnel operations began in April 1865 by contractors George Thomson & Co. of Cheltenham, with a workforce rising to 1074. Seven shafts (eventually eight) were sunk, to speed the task in two directions. The 1851m (2024yd) tunnel was essentially completed in 1867 and the line opened on 1 February 1870.

Where the path meets a crossing track, turn left to take the track across an open area. (*Take care and observe the usual courtesies over the next section through the golf course.)* After about 100m the track runs into a wooded area with raised ground to the left before reaching the signed Bell Hole tee on the left and green workshop building ahead.

F Turn right in front of the workshop and, after about 50m, turn left to take a red grit path that soon winds to the right across flat ground. Look for a white gatepost in a line of trees ahead and cross to it at the point where the path is closest. At the gatepost, bear diagonally right, looking for an opening in the bushes about 150m away. At the opening, go down the steps, cross the brook and then head diagonally left over an open area to another opening between trees that leads back onto the golf course. Ahead is a track, which soon becomes grassed, that leads across a fairway to some small trees. You will pass a white painted marker on your right before coming to a second fairway. Cross this and head for the footpath sign at the edge of the course. Here follow the route round to the left into a driveway that leads to a road (Bradway Road). **See Bradway.**

BRADWAY: In Bradway Road you follow what was once the Greenhill Moor (later Owler Bar) Turnpike as far as the top of Twentywell Lane, where there was a tollbar. Before that, opposite The Bradway pub and right over the tunnel, is a small brick building with an odd history. Thomson s the tunnel contractors built the original front part as a school for the navvy children encamped nearby. The United Methodist Free Church used it for Sunday services and retained it when the families moved on. Extended, it now serves community purposes.

G Turn left and walk for about 300m before crossing and turning right into Twentywell Lane. Descend the 1km to the junction with Abbeydale Road South. *The deep cutting on the left after Twentywell Road contains the northern entrance to the Bradway Tunne*l. Cross the road with care and go directly ahead and take the path on the left of the signed public bridleway (Water Lane), which soon passes sports fields on the left before opening into Cavendish Avenue. **See Water Lane.**

WATER LANE: From Abbeydale Road South, Water Lane looks like a typical holloway with a causey alongside. The name originally meant a way leading to a stream. Dore, with its now culverted brook running off the moor and its well on the Green, hardly needed a lane just to the Sheaf, though you could go on to Bradway and Norton. So the name may have been given to the track used by the people of Ashfurlong hamlet to fetch water, later to be applied to most of the rest of what is now Ashfurlong Road. Other theories are invited!

Go to the top of this road and then follow the signed path ahead on the right of a driveway until it comes to a road (Burlington Grove). Here turn left, walk about 60m and then take the signed path on the right. This runs between gardens and allotments for about 250m before reaching a kissing gate Turn left here (Vicarage Lane) and soon pass the Village Green on the left before reaching the Old School ahead.

Dronfield Church

Part of an inscription on a gravestone in Dronfield churchyard

TOTLEY MOSS AND LONGSHAW

With excellent distant views in all directions, this walk is worth saving for a fine day with good visibility. It passes a number of sites with significant local history.

DISTANCE 15km (9¼ miles)

MINIMUM TIME 4½ hours

TERRAIN Good paths and some rougher, but not difficult, sections

LANDSCAPE Woodland and open moorland

START/FINISH Old School, Dore

PARKING On road in Dore

PUBLIC TOILETS At Longshaw Visitor Centre (when open) and Fox House

REFRESHMENTS Two pubs (Devonshire Arms and Hare & Hounds) and a cafe in Dore. At Longshaw and Fox House Inn

TRAINS & BUSES Bus services 30, 65, 98, 214 and 240

Route Directions

A Facing the front of the Old School, exit through a gateway at the left corner of the building and turn right to pass the church. At the T-junction, turn left into Church Lane and continue until you see Old Hay Gardens on the right. After a further 80m, cross a stile ahead on the right to take the public footpath that goes downhill in the field parallel to the road. Leave the field at the bottom corner near the road.

B Go along Avenue Farm drive with the brook (Oldhay Brook) soon visible on the left. **See Oldhay and Avenue Farm.** Continue towards a metal gate and pass into the field with the brook on the left. Continue ahead, passing through a narrow gate close to the brook and, after a further 50m beside the brook, turn right up the field with a wire fence on your right. Pass through the gate on to the metalled road (Shorts Lane).

C Turn left and continue along the road that within 50m becomes a rough track with a sharp bend to the right signposted 'Public Bridleway to Blacka Moor'.

OLDHAY AND AVENUE FARM: Oldhay was a major industrial site. A big lead smelting mill was at work by 1585 and continued until the early 19th century. Later it was a scythe grinding wheel. A short distance upstream, by Avenue Farm, a paper mill was operating in 1721 and possibly in 1650. In the 1830s it was a forge for manufacturing scythe blades and the two concerns merged. Totley Forge became Tyzack's Forge and Joshua Tyzack converted it into Avenue Farm in 1891.

Go along this bridleway and soon pass through stone gateposts by a board indicating Blacka Moor Nature Reserve. Continue ahead on the bridleway and after another 200m with the stream on the left, the track forks.

D Take the left hand track that goes downhill to cross the stream. This then continues uphill and, after about 500m, the woodland thins out, the gradient

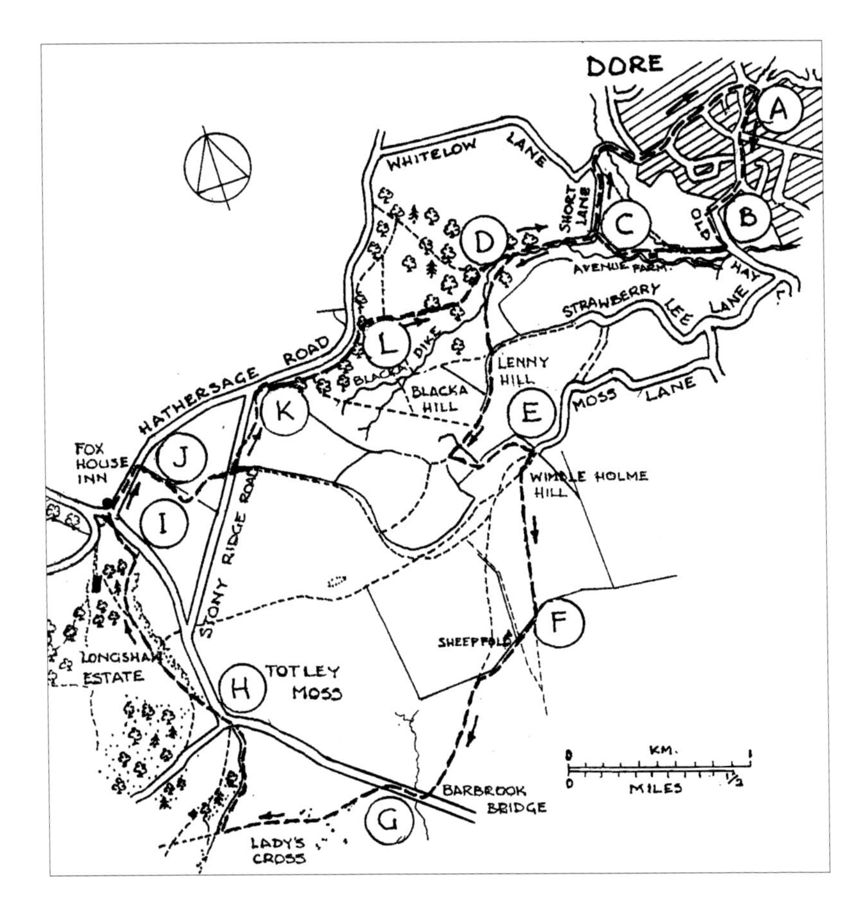

slackens, and the track passes through a gap in a wall and is joined by another track coming uphill from the left. Bearing right, continue up a stony bridleway for about 800m, coming to a large gate with a smaller gate on the left. You are now in the area known as Strawberry Lee. **See Strawberry Lee Grange**.

Go through the gate and turn left on to a path with a fence on the left. Cross the plank bridge and go through the gate ahead. Turn left on to a narrow gently rising path that can be slippery in wet conditions. A broken wall and a wire fence appear on the left. Continue ahead to meet a broad, vehicle-rutted track.

STRAWBERRY LEE GRANGE: Beauchief Abbey was founded about 1176, when Premonstratensians or White Canons (who started at PrØmontrØn Northern France) arrived here from Welbeck. Land was donated to them in stages and Strawberry Lee came their way sometime before 1250. A grange was an outlying farm, in this case a sheep farm. The Canons were a working order and sheep provided a major part of their income.

E Turn right up the broad track for 60m then, from where you can see the main track curve right, take the grassy track that forks left. Continue on this gently rising track, passing a pink gas pipeline marker on your left. Soon after the track levels out, about 800m from point E, there is another gas pipeline marker where you also meet the foundations of a ruined wall crossing the track.

F Turn right, go up the path along the left side of the wall remains. At the summit of the hill, cross another track beside another gas pipeline marker. Continue along the wall, soon passing the ruins of a sheepfold and a pair of gateposts on the right. After another 200m the wall you are following bends right. Follow it for a further 90m to where a path crosses it. Turn left along this path, going gently downhill to a kissing gate in the wall. Cross the road, turn right and take the path by the road for 200m to a bridge (Bar Brook).

Lady's Cross

G Continue and after 35m turn left over a ladder stile with a finger post indicating a public footpath. Take this path, that rises gently, and look out for Lady's Cross, off to the left after about 400m. Having had a look at the cross, return to the path and continue uphill. Soon after the summit there are gates in a wire fence ahead. Just before these gates, turn right on to a grassy track. Continue with a fence on your left and over a stile to the road.

H Cross the road and go through the large white gate beside the 'National Trust – Wooden Pole' sign. The similar white gate leading to White Edge Lodge should be behind you. Go ahead on a broad grassy track. **See Greenhill Moor Turnpike.** Pass the stone steps going up to the right and, later, a small quarry also on the right. Continue on the path with the wall on your left until you reach a gateway leading into the woods and to a car park.

GREENHILL MOOR TURNPIKE: Past the white gate you enter a former turnpike road and soon an older one coming from the left. This was the Hathersage branch of the Greenhill Moor Turnpike. Authorized in 1781, that ran from the original Chesterfield Turnpike at Dyche Lane to Calver along the line of today's B6054 and A625. The short stretch you were on first was added later to avoid a sharp turn. New 19th century roads enabled the Duke of Rutland to close these to the public.

I Walk through the car park near its upper boundary wall and leave it via a gap in the wall at the far right-hand corner, taking a path in the woods parallel to the road.

The Longshaw National Trust Visitor Centre, with refreshments and toilets, can be reached using the path leading from the lower side of the car park. Opening hours are restricted in the winter months.

Take the right fork to the gate and on to the road at Fox House Inn. Go 300m along the road towards Sheffield, to a footpath sign on your right.

J Once over the ladder stile, take the path ahead beside a wall. After 200m, this path swings right then back left to cross the wall at gateposts. Continue to a ladder stile, cross the road and turn left on to roadside path. After 50m, pass a wall, at right angles to the road, and a stone pillar. After another 50m, turn right between boulders, at a rough lay-by, to join an old road that runs alongside the main road and meets it again at the road junction.

K Go right, along the road to Sheffield, for about 80m to a car parking area near the corner of a wood. From the car park, take the path through a gap in the wall, into the wood, and on a line parallel to the road. Cross a small stream on a railway sleeper bridge and, after another 300m, pass through a gate. Continue on this path, meeting a signed bridleway after 200m near a Blacka Moor Nature Reserve notice. **See Blacka Moor Nature Reserve.**

BLACKA MOOR NATURE RESERVE: The Reserve, 181ha (447 acres), includes Blacka Plantation, Lenny Hill, Strawberry Lea, Blacka Hill and Bole Hill. It was part of the Rutland estates sold in 1927 after the death of the 8th Duke. Later Alderman J. G. Graves acquired it and bequeathed it to Sheffield in 1933 through the Graves Charitable Trust. The object was 'to preserve the moor in its natural state and to prevent any alterations to its present character'. It became a reserve in 1993.

L Turn right on the bridleway to descend through woodland. Cross a signposted public footpath after about 100m, and continue on a bridleway down a steepening slope. Pass through a gate and continue downhill. Soon after the bridleway levels out, pass a bridge on the left, signed 'Bridleway to Devil's Elbow Road', and continue ahead. Pass through a gate, and continue ahead on the bridleway to Shorts Lane, passing between gateposts to meet a bridleway joining from your right.

D Continue ahead until, after 600m, the track turns sharp left. You will soon arrive at C. The fingerpost on the right shows the path you came up on the outward route. Pass it and continue on Shorts Lane to the T-junction. Turn right here along the road (Whitelow Lane) crossing a stream and then uphill, to pass Newfield Lane on the left. Continue ahead to Townhead Rd and onwards to the village centre. At the road with the Hare & Hounds pub ahead, cross, turn left and then right to take Savage Lane to reach the Old School 70m on the right.

Cattle at Longshaw

HOUNDKIRK AND PORTER BROOK

A walk providing extensive views down the Sheaf valley from the Houndkirk Road, followed by the very different scenery of the Porter Brook valley.

DISTANCE	14km (9 miles)
MINIMUM TIME	4 hours
TERRAIN	Mostly good paths but the section over Houndkirk Moor requires care
LANDSCAPE	Mainly moorland and woodland
START/FINISH	Old School, Dore
PARKING	On road in Dore
PUBLIC TOILETS	Forge Dam
REFRESHMENTS	Two pubs (Devonshire Arms and Hare & Hounds) and a cafe in Dore. The Alpaca Centre and pub at Ringinglow, Forge Dam and (off the route) the W.O.R.K. Centre at Bents Green (not Sundays)
TRAINS & BUSES	Bus services 30, 84, 98, 284 and M17 Other services, eg 83, serve Bents Green

This walk includes the old Houndkirk Road, now classed as a public byway. At weekends the road is used by cars and motorbikes, so you may wish to do the walk on a weekday to avoid the traffic.

Route Directions

A Leave the Old School yard by the large gateway, turn left (Savage Lane) and walk up towards the village centre. At the junction (High Street) turn left, then cross the road into Townhead Road and continue for about 700m. At the end of Townhead Road continue ahead along Whitelow Lane. The road descends then climbs for about 1½km (1 mile) to reach Hathersage Road. At the junction, carefully cross the road aiming for the public footpath sign, climb the steps and go through the gate to enter moorland (Houndkirk Moor).

B The path climbs diagonally left, then right, first through bracken, then heather to a concrete marker post. Pause here to consider your next steps as the way ahead is not clear!

The path marked on OS maps goes straight ahead but is often very wet and the heather is being trampled by walkers trying to avoid the boggy sections. The following route should reduce these problems.

C Leave the marker post by the path that follows a line slightly to the left of the line by which you approached. Continue, looking back at the post occasionally to check that you are maintaining the same line. After about 200m, look for a second concrete post, about 250m away, which is to the right of the line you are walking. Continue on the path, which now bears gently to the right, to pass close to the second

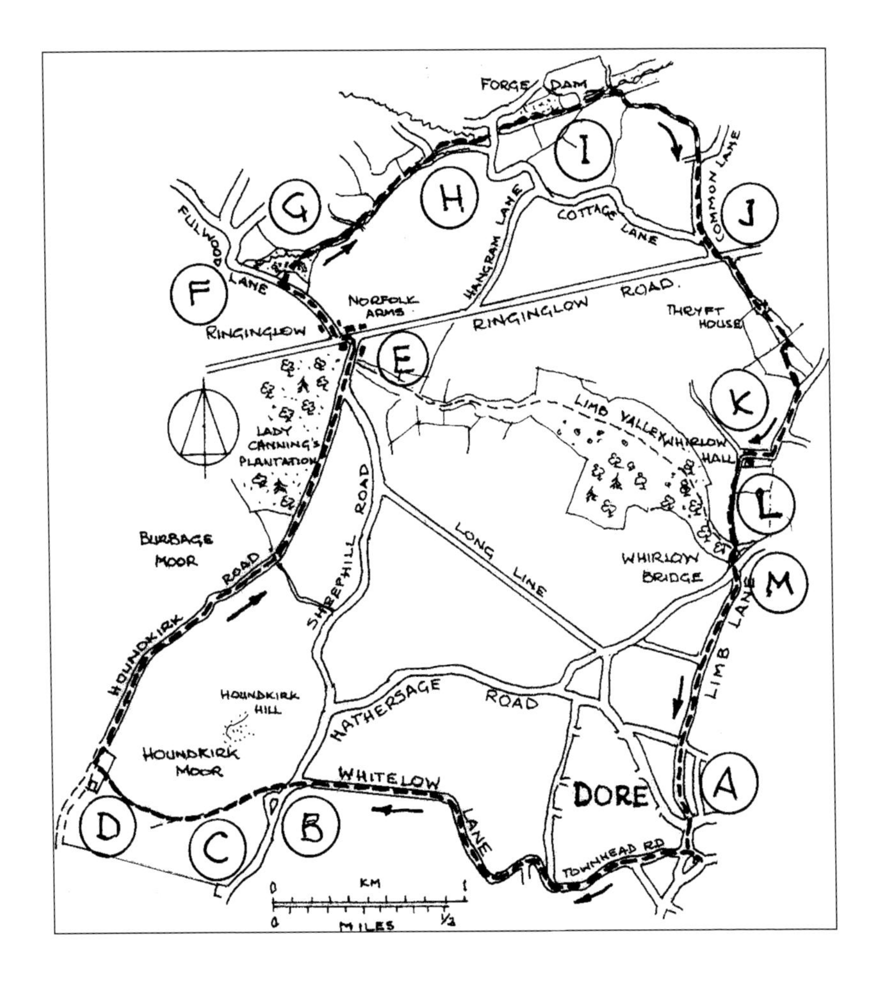

concrete post. At this post, look straight ahead just below the skyline, to locate a public footpath sign. The path you are on leads directly to this sign that is on the well-used byway (Houndkirk Road). **See Houndkirk.**

D Turn right along the wide track and follow it for 2km (1¼ miles). Enjoy views over the city to the Don Valley beyond, passing an old mile post and then Lady Canning's Plantation on your left, to reach Sheephill Road. Turn left on to this road and continue ahead to The Round House and The Norfolk Arms. **See Ringinglow.**

HOUNDKIRK: Houndkirk Moor is named after the hill which according to antiquarian S.O.Addy means 'giant's church'. *Ent* is Old English for giant and the name used to be pronounced Ankirk. This may appear far-fetched, but if after passing the hill you look back from Houndkirk Road to its north-west face you will perhaps see Addy's point. An ancient saltway, this road formed a section of the Sheffield-Buxton Turnpike, authorized in 1758, until 1825. It had been superseded by the less bleak and arduous Dore Turnpike (Hathersage Road) of 1818.

E Turn left and then immediately right along Fulwood Lane picking up the Sheffield Round Walk signs. Pass Mayfield Alpacas Visitor Centre on your right. Just before Moorfield Farm on your left, turn right into a rough parking area, again signposted as the Sheffield Round Walk, and leave by the far left corner using steps to a footbridge.

RINGINGLOW: After 1758 Ringinglow formed the junction of turnpike roads from Sheffield to Sparrowpit (for Manchester) via Hathersage and Hope, and to Buxton via Grindleford and Tideswell. On enclosure of the commons the Round House was built as a toll-house (1795) and around 1800 the Ringinglow Inn - later the Norfolk Arms - was opened. A wire mill on Fulwood Lane operated from 1844 to the 1860s.

F Turn right and follow the stream (Porter Brook). **See Porter Brook.** After a while the path leaves the wooded area and proceeds with a field on the left and the brook further away to your right. Cross over a lane and go through a squeeze stile opposite by the public footpath sign.

PORTER BROOK: The woodland around Porter Brook is The Clough, famed as the most likely location of Fulwood Spa. In 1661 there was concern about actual or potential plague victims visiting it. Seventy years later it figured in a history of South Yorkshire and Derbyshire spas. Muriel Hall assembled the evidence for The Rough, on the eastern side of The Clough, in her little book *The Mayfield Valley* (1972). The spa s healing properties, from chalybeate which eventually disappeared, may have arisen from coal workings at Ringinglow.

G Keep to the right of the fence and follow a woodland path. At first the stream is on your right but cross as signposted over a bridge, then downhill with the stream on your left. You then arrive at a point where there is a bridge across the stream on your left. Go across the bridge and continue upwards with a field fence on your left, then downhill and through a stile to a junction of lanes.

The Round House, Ringinglow

H Cross over and go straight ahead following the Sheffield Round Walk sign through a gap in the wall and follow the path with a fence on your left; the stream is now on your right. Pass over a bridge, go up the bank, join the path coming in from your right and turn left to the road. Cross over the road, pass a green barrier and follow a wide path with the stream on your left. Cross the stream by the footbridge on your left and walk round Forge Dam. **See Forge Dam.**

FORGE DAM: The original forge,Whiteley Wood Forge, was important for its association with Thomas Boulsover, who built it. In 1743 he discovered how to plate copper with silver. He was no great entrepreneur and was content to make silverplated buttons and, some say, snuffboxes. They were buffed (polished) at a mill up the Mayfield Valley. Joseph Hancock pioneered more ambitious articles of Old Sheffield Plate in the 1750s, though not here. The grassy area opposite the playground marks the site of another dam.

I Continue round the Dam and at the far end go through the gate and down the slope where you will find a cafe and toilets. Continue on the main path with the play area on your left. Shortly bear left (ignoring the first public bridleway sign on your right). Then turn first right uphill following a public bridleway sign. Walk up the lane to reach the road at the top (ignoring a public footpath sign on your right part way along the lane). Go straight ahead up the road (Common Lane) to reach its junction with Ringinglow Road. Turn left and continue for about 50m.

To visit the W.O.R.K. Centre for refreshment, go for a further 60m, then turn left and follow the signs to the Centre, which provides educational and vocational training for adults with learning difficulties. Well worth the detour.

J Turn left, cross the road, and take the public footpath on the right after about 50m. Look for the sign *Thryft House* on the gatepost as you follow a tarmac drive. Pass to the right of the cottages, keeping straight ahead as the drive swings left. At the entrance to Thryft Farm House, follow the tarmac track as it veers to the right. When the track swings left, go straight ahead through a wooden gate signposted *Whirlow Trails* and, after a second wooden gate, follow a field path through another gate passing to the right of a lonely tree on a clear path.

K Go through the gate at the end and turn right onto the road beyond. Follow this road, carrying straight on at the T-junction with Whirlow Lane on the left. Bear right following the road up to Whirlow Hall Farm, keeping the farm buildings on your left. **See Whirlow Hall Farm.**

WHIRLOW HALL FARM: Whirlow means the mound on the boundary. It is hard to pinpoint the mound; the boundary is the Limb Brook. Whirlow Hall and its farm are on an old packhorse trail from Sheffield via Dore to the Baslow area. The Hall was the original seat of the Bright family (15th century till about 1718). It was rebuilt in 1843 from an Elizabethan predecessor. The farmhouse is 17th century. All this is now owned by Sheffield City Council and administered by the Whirlow Hall Farm Trust, a children's charity.

Whirlow Hall Farm

L Beyond the farm turn left through a steel gate following a public bridleway sign along an attractive enclosed path. Ignore the stile on your right. Keep straight ahead with a wall on your left passing intriguing stone steps on your left and right (part of Whinfell Quarry Garden) to emerge in the lay-by at Whirlow Bridge. **See Whirlow Bridge.**

M Turn right, cross the road to join Limb Lane and return to the village.

WHIRLOW BRIDGE: The bit of road passing the entrance to Whirlow Brook Park was the main road until the 1950s. It crosses Whirlow Bridge, said to have a concealed datestone of 1816 and replacing a ford through Limb Brook. This formed the historic boundary between Northumbria and Mercia, Yorkshire and Derbyshire (till 1935) and the provinces of York and Canterbury (till 1974). There was a pub here for nearly a century until posh incomers stopped the licence. The City bought Whirlow Brook (c.1906) in 1946, soon after acquiring the neighbouring woods.

Mayfield Alpacas

THE HOUNDKIRK ROAD

The Houndkirk Road, a major relic from days when travel was a tiring and risky business, today provides us with a superb platform from which to view the Sheaf Valley and well beyond.

DISTANCE	14½km (9 miles)
MINIMUM TIME	4 hours
TERRAIN	Some road walking, 3km (2 miles) on Houndkirk Road, moorland and woodland
LANDSCAPE	Extensive views of moorland, Dore and Sheffield
START/FINISH	Old School, Dore
PARKING	On road in Dore
PUBLIC TOILETS	None on route
REFRESHMENTS	Two pubs (Devonshire Arms and Hare & Hounds) and a cafe in Dore; Norfolk Arms, Fox House, Cricket Inn and Crown Inn (all off route)
TRAINS & BUSES	Services 30, 98 and M17

Route Directions

A Leave the Old School yard by the large gateway, cross the road (Savage Lane) and turn left. Walk up towards the village centre. At the junction (High Street) turn right and, passing the Methodist Church on the right and the Devonshire Arms on the left, go to the staggered crossroads. Continue ahead into Rushley Road (it becomes Limb Lane) and continue for approximately 750m, passing the entrance to Ecclesall Woods car park on the right and an unnamed lane on the left, to reach Ash House Lane on the left. Turn left and walk up this road to the junction with the main road (Hathersage Road). Turn left, continue for 150m to the crossroads and turn right into Long Line.

B Walk up Long Line (no pavement) for about 1km (two-thirds of a mile), looking out for a red Post Office box mounted on a telegraph pole on the left. About 100m past this box, turn right on to a signed public footpath opposite house number 155. Pass through the left-hand side of the gate and walk along the drive. At the gated entrance to Barberfields Farm, take the path half-left between the properties.

Before the next gate, turn left on a grass track, go through a gate on the right and turn left on to a farm track between two fields. Walk ahead towards a row of fir trees on the left. At three metal gates, take the small left hand gate into a large field. Walk half left across the field (no distinct path) towards a wooden stile in a wall immediately to the right of a line of hawthorn trees running along the top of the field.

Go over the stile as sign-posted and proceed with a wall on the left to another stile into woodland.

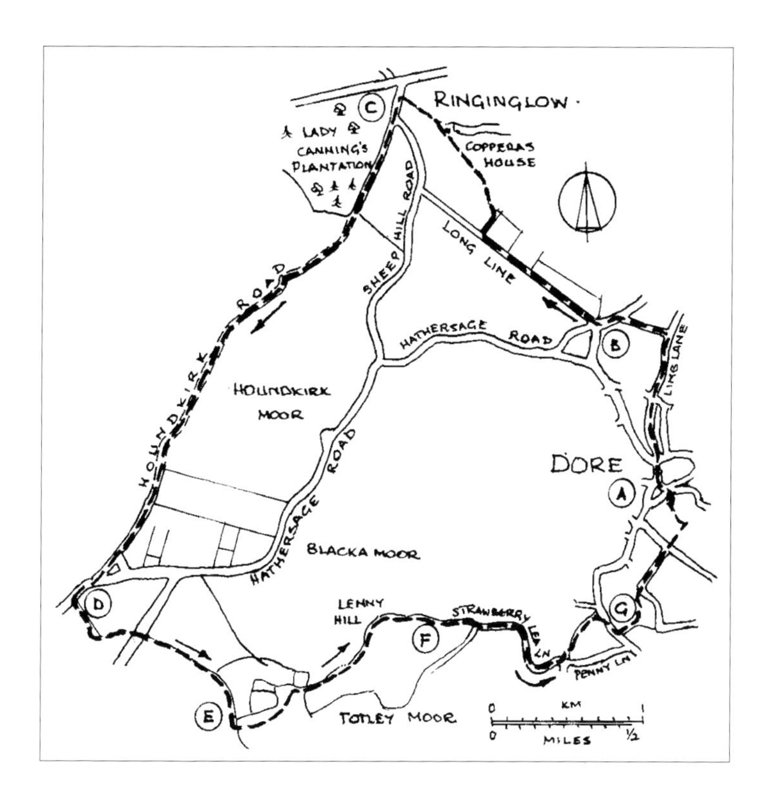

Continue with the wall on the left for 15m, through another stile and follow the faint path ahead. Cross the stream by the stone footbridge and continue over laid stones and a grassy area to the T-junction of paths. Turn left, now with decaying buildings (Copperas House) on your left, to more laid stones through a boggy area. Follow the footpath sign over a stream and then the well-defined path uphill to reach a stile and join a road (Sheephill Road).

C Turn left, walk past Moor Cottage and, where Sheephill Road starts to bend to the left, cross the road to a public byway signpost at the start of an unmade track (Houndkirk Road). Walk up this track for 600m to reach a gate. Go through this and continue for a further 2¾km (1¾ miles) to reach another gate. **See Houndkirk.**

HOUNDKIRK: Houndkirk Moor is named after the hill which according to antiquarian S.O. Addy means giant s church . *Ent* is Old English for giant and the name used to be pronounced Ankirk. This may appear far-fetched, but if on approaching the hill you look at its north-west face you will perhaps see Addy s point. An ancient saltway, this road formed a section of the Sheffield-Buxton Turnpike, authorized in 1758, until 1825, having been superseded by the less bleak and arduous Dore Turnpike (Hathersage Road) of 1818.

The views from this part of the route are excellent in many directions, so make the most of them, especially if the visibility is good. At the second gate, cross the drive leading to buildings to the right and continue ahead for about 250m to reach a road (Hathersage Road). Cross the road, turn right and continue for about 150m to reach a footpath sign on the left.

The Houndkirk Road

D Go over the ladder stile and follow a well-defined path across the field, immediately to the right of a boundary wall, before veering right then swinging left to reach a ladder stile at the next road (A625). Cross the road and go through the wooden gate by a public bridleway sign and continue for about 1km (two-thirds of a mile).

E About 50m before a white vertical gas pipeline marker (you will have passed a similar marker earlier), leave the track and go through a gate followed by a stile over a wall on your left. For 500m the path follows the left-hand side of a shallow valley, with Dore and Sheffield ahead, to join a wider path. Turn right at the junction, soon pass a Peak and Northern Footpath Society sign and, after a further 25 yards, go through a gate and enter Blacka Moor Nature Reserve. The path descends through mixed woodland and eventually reaches a junction of paths. Your route is to the right, but read first the inscription on the bench.

F Follow this track down through the reserve; the memorial to Stephen Morton is just off the track on the right after about 25m. The track flattens and goes over a footbridge before arriving at a gate into the informal car park for the nature reserve. Continue ahead on the metalled road to its junction with Lane Head Road. Go ahead on Penny Lane but immediately turn left as directed by the public footpath sign and walk past some cottages. Opposite the farm buildings turn right down the track where directed by a yellow arrow and over a stone stile into the field. Turn left along the field edge and walk towards a house, with a stile immediately behind it. Go over the stile, down steps and along the drive, respecting the owner's privacy. At the end of the drive, turn right (Old Hay Lane) and walk for 150m to a footpath sign on the left beside a wall.

G Go over the stile with a wall on your right, follow the path to a kissing gate, go over the first brook (Needham's Dike) and then turn left to take the footbridge over Oldhay Brook. Follow the left path uphill with the brook on your left. Climb the stone steps and follow the path up across the field and past a seat, to a tarmac path in the top left corner of the field. Turn right along this path and, at its end, turn left and walk along the road (Totley Brook Road) to reach a T-junction (Furniss Avenue). Cross to a footpath opposite, signposted to Kingswood Day Nursery, and follow this straight ahead to Busheywood Road. Turn left into Savage Lane and follow this up to the Old School.

DORE BOUNDARY WALK

This walk follows, as closely as possible, the boundary of the old township of Dore. It offers a very wide variety of scenery and views, much historical interest - and a challenge!
It has been split into two walks, both starting in Dore, which can be combined to give a single walk of about 18km (11 miles).

PART 1

DISTANCE	9km (5½ miles)
MINIMUM TIME	2½ hours
TERRAIN	Pavements, easy field paths and unsurfaced tracks
LANDSCAPE	Woodland and suburban streets
START/FINISH	Old School, Dore
PARKING	On road in Dore
PUBLIC TOILETS	None on route
REFRESHMENTS	Two pubs (Devonshire Arms and Hare & Hounds) and a cafe in Dore, Abbeydale Garden Centre, Seasons cafe on Abbeydale Road South, Cricket Inn and Crown Inn (the last two are slightly off route)
TRAINS & BUSES	Bus services 30, 65, 84, 214, 240, 272 and 284

Route Directions

A Leave the Old School yard by the large gateway, cross the road (Savage Lane) and turn left. Walk up towards the village centre. At the junction (High Street) turn right, passing the Methodist Church on the right and the Devonshire Arms on the left, and soon reach a staggered crossroads. Continue ahead into Rushley Road and follow this road, which becomes Limb Lane, for nearly 1½km (1 mile) to reach the main Hathersage Road at Whirlow Bridge.

B At this junction, cross Limb Lane and then turn right down the signed path and, bearing right, pass into the open area. Keeping the brook (Limb Brook) on your left, pass the ruins of the Whirlow Wheel, 50m to your left, before, in due course, reaching the lower left hand corner of the field with a stile in the wall ahead.

Whirlow Wheel

Cross the stile, bear right along the stone-edged path and after 100m at a signed junction of paths continue

t

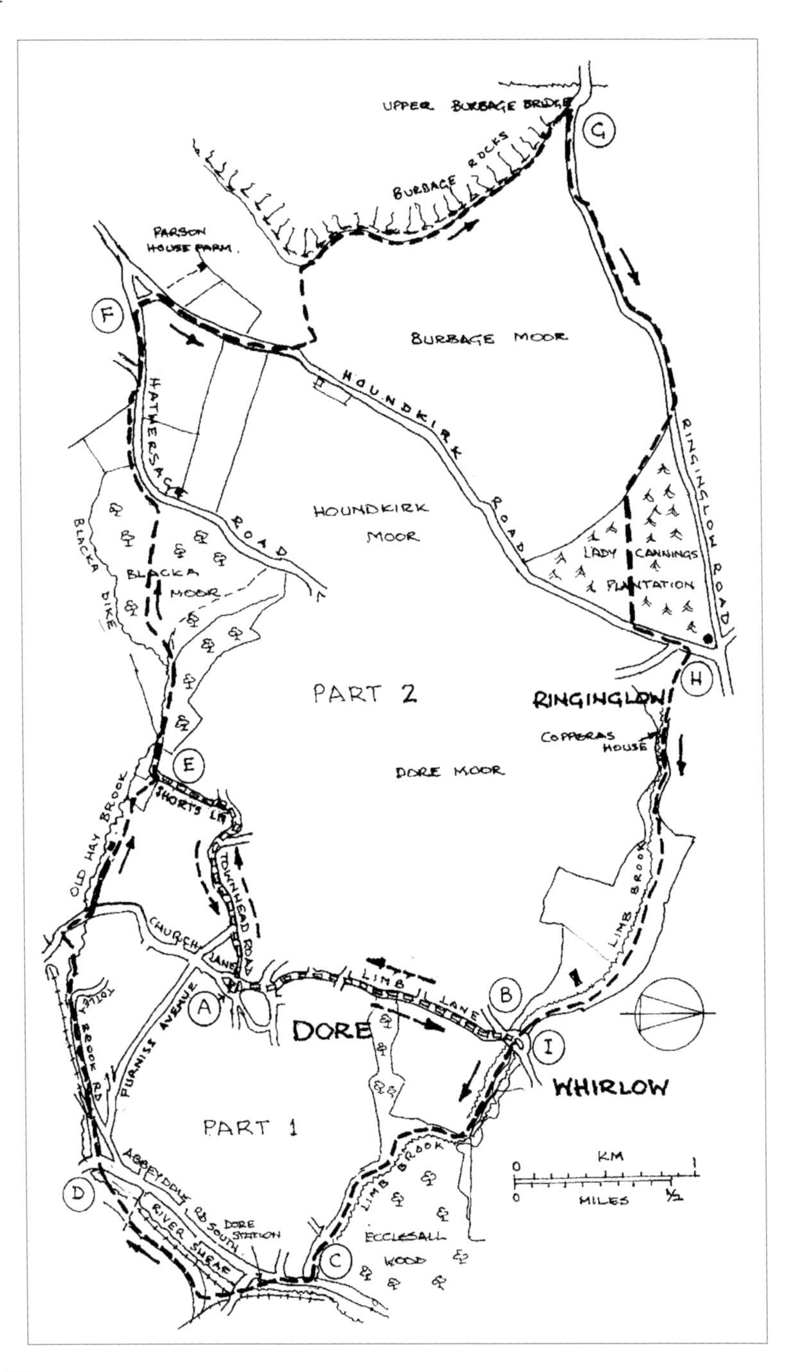
UPPER BURBAGE BRIDGE
G
BURBAGE ROCKS
PARSON HOUSE FARM
F
BURBAGE MOOR
HOUNDKIRK ROAD
HATHERSAGE ROAD
RINGINGLOW ROAD
HOUNDKIRK MOOR
LADY CANNINGS PLANTATION
BLACKA DIKE
BLACKA MOOR
H
PART 2
RINGINGLOW
COPPERAS HOUSE
E
DORE MOOR
SHORTS LN
OLD HAY BROOK
TOWNHEAD ROAD
CHURCH LANE
LIMB LANE
LIMB BROOK
A
B
DORE
FURNISS AVENUE
TOTLEY BROOK RD
I
WHIRLOW
PART 1
KM
0
1
MILES
½
ABBEYDALE RD SOUTH
D
RIVER SHEAF
DORE STATION
ECCLESALL WOOD
C

straight ahead on the stone-edged path following the sign to Abbeydale Road South. Cross several sleeper bridges and then at a T-junction of paths at a gate, turn left. The site of Ryecroft Mill is to the right shortly before you reach this T-junction. **See Ryecroft Mill.** Then follow this bridleway for about 1km (two-thirds of a mile) with the brook on your left, right down to the main road (Abbeydale Road South) at Limb Bridge.

RYECROFT MILL: Known also as Limb Mill, Ryecroft Mill is first mentioned in 1658 in a deed of sale. It was then a lead mill called the Lym Smyltinge and Edward Ash of Tidsalle (Tideswell) was the tenant. By the start of the 19th century it was a corn mill popularly known as Jacky Mill, doubtless after the miller, John Unwin. By 1871 it had closed. Stone from the mill house was used to build the nearby cottage. Plenty of traces survive, e.g. the dam, some goits and the wheel pit.

C Cross the road, turn right and, after nearly 200m, turn left into the station yard and head for the right hand corner of the old station building, where a path will take you to a road (Twentywell Lane).Cross the road, turn left to cross the first bridge and then turn right on a public footpath over a stile and then continue ahead. Having climbed to a more open grassed area, keep to the right hand fence to take the path into woodland (Poynton Wood). This path, with the railway down to your right, largely follows the contour, to cross a paved path with rails after about 500m. Continue ahead, passing blocks of flat on your right, and drop down to a bridge over a brook and into Mill Lane, which leads to the dual carriageway (Baslow Road).

D Cross this road and enter Grove Road, on the right of the Methodist Church. After about 250m, take the footbridge over the railway and then turn left at the road (Totley Brook Road). Follow this until, just before the right hand curve, continue on the signed track on the left over the brook (Oldhay Brook). Where a path over a bridge joins from the right, bear left and continue through a kissing gate to the road (Old Hay Lane). Here, turn right and, after 150m, take the first drive on the left. Just past the garages on the right, take the half-hidden path on the right, to cross the brook and up steps. At the top, turn left into the drive to Avenue Farm, which soon passes houses on the left and leads to a gate into a field. Continue with the brook to the left and pass through a gated stile before bearing right uphill with a wire fence on your right to reach a lane.

At this point it is possible to join the walks together. Turn left here and then follow the Route Instructions for Part 2, starting at point E on the next page.

Oldhay Brook

E Continue the Part 1 walk by turning right along the metalled lane (Shorts Lane) to the T-junction with a white-gated drive ahead. Turn right here along the road (Whitelow Lane) crossing a stream and then uphill, to pass Newfield Lane on the left. Continue ahead to Townhead Rd and onwards to the village centre. You will soon see the Hare & Hounds pub ahead. Cross the road, turn left then right and take Savage Lane to reach the Old School 70m on the right.

PART 2

DISTANCE	15km (9 miles)
MINIMUM TIME	4 hours
TERRAIN	Easy field paths, unsurfaced tracks and rough moorland paths. A steady climb in Blacka
LANDSCAPE	Woodland, open moorland and urban roads. Good views of the Sheaf valley and the moors to the west
START/FINISH	Old School, Dore
PARKING	On road in Dore
PUBLIC TOILETS	None on route
REFRESHMENTS	See Part 1 for refreshments in Dore, Fox House Inn (700m off route), Norfolk Arms (off route) and Whirlow Brook Hall
TRAINS & BUSES	Bus services 30, 65, 84, 214, 240, 272 and 284

Route Directions

See Part 1 of this walk for the map.

A Leave the Old School yard by the large gateway, turn left (Savage Lane) and walk uphill towards the village centre. At the junction with High Street, turn left and then cross the road into Townhead Road on the right and continue for about 700m. At the end of Townhead Road continue down Whitelow Lane. The road first descends to cross a bridge. About 100m past this bridge, turn left into Shorts Lane and continue for about 400m, almost to the end of the straight section.

This is the point where the Part 1 walk joins from the left.

E Continue ahead and soon bear right to follow the bridleway. Ignoring any paths and tracks going left or right, continue through the Blacka Moor Nature Reserve. The path narrows and then climbs, initially through woodland, for about 800m to a small grass area with a signpost, where there is an excellent view down the Sheaf valley and beyond. Continue ahead and, just before the road, turn left on to the path running parallel to the road. Follow this for about 500m until it passes through a wall into a small parking area. On the opposite side of the road was the site of Piper House. **See Piper House.**

Turn left at the roadside, cross the A625 to Froggatt and continue ahead towards Hathersage for about 400m.

PIPER HOUSE: The Rev Henry Hunt Piper (d. 1864) was the nonconformist chaplain of the Shore family of Norton Hall and also ran a prestigious private school. When the Dore commons were enclosed Samuel Shore Jr. was awarded two pieces of land. He sold one of them, a five-acre plot at Houndkirk, to Piper, who built two cottages there. In the 1841 census they were called Houndkirk Lodge, but Piper House was already current too. They were dismantled within living memory.

F Here, cross the road, take the drive ahead to Parson House and, after 150m, turn right on to the unmade byway (Houndkirk Road). **See Parson House.** This climbs gently for about 750m to reach a summit with two small orange gas pipeline markers.

PARSON HOUSE: Enclosure Commissioners were empowered to sell land to defray administrative costs. In 1811 moorlands in Dore and Hathersage were auctioned. An enormous tract of over 500 acres on the north-west side of Houndkirk Road was sold to Thomas Bingham, incumbent of Norbury, for about £650. Multiply by 50 for a 2008 sum. The Duke of Rutland subsequently bought it. The future site of Parson House was on its south-western boundary. The name first occurs on the 1840 OS map, though Bingham s House appears in 1851.

Here, bear left to take the track between the heather for 100m. At the junction with another path, turn left and continue for 350m to another path junction with marker post and cairns. Turn right here and then follow this path for about 2km (1¼ miles) along the Edge to reach a stile by the roadside (Upper Burbage Bridge).

G Turn right and follow this road – the left hand verge is walkable for most of the way – for 1¾km (1 mile) until you reach a wood (Lady Canning's Plantation) on the right. **See Lady Canning's Plantation**.

LADY CANNING S PLANTATION: Lady Joan Canning was the widow of George Canning, a friend of the Devonshires. He had a distinguished career in foreign affairs before becoming Prime Minister in 1827, but died after just four months in office. Presumably at the 1811 auction, he bought two large allotments bordered by the Ox Stones, Limb Brook and Houndkirk Road 213 acres for £589 5s 4d. The eastern one became the plantation. In *Across the Derbyshire Moors* (24 editions, 1904-46) it was labelled luckless . It looks healthier now.

Turn right here and follow the track, with the wood on your left, for 350m before taking the stile on your left into the wood. Follow this curving path for nearly 1km, eventually to emerge back at Houndkirk Road. Turn left here and, at the junction with a road (Sheephill Road), turn left and continue for about 100m before taking a stile on the right.

H Keeping the brook on your left, head down the field towards its lower left hand corner.

Copperas House

After passing the ruins of Copperas House on the right, a gate on the right leads to a footpath passing down through the woods for about 2km (1¼ miles). **See Copperas House.**

COPPERAS HOUSE: Yellow crystals, iron pyrites or fool s gold, were present in the Ringinglow coal. From this mixture, popularly called dross, copperas (aka ferrous sulphate or green vitriol) was manufactured here around 1815-60. The dross was laid on slabs behind the ruined building and ex posed to the air and rain. A whitish acid ran off, was collected in a cistern, pumped into a copper and boiled with scrap iron for 5-6 days. The resultant solution was sold in casks as a mordant for fixing dyes.

About halfway through these woods, the path divides; the right branch crosses a bridge and leads to Whirlow Brook Hall, where refreshments are available. The left hand branch takes you directly to the lay-by at Whirlow Bridge.

I Turn right here and walk to the end of the lay-by, cross Hathersage Road into Limb Lane and follow this back to the village.

Burbage Brook

DORE TO HATHERSAGE

A superb moorland walk with wonderful views and plenty of history. Pick a fine day for this one and see the Peak District at its best. Come back by train or bus.

DISTANCE	9km (5½ miles)
MINIMUM TIME	2½-3 hours
TERRAIN	Good paths and tracks; Houndkirk Moor requires care
LANDSCAPE	Moorland and woodland
START	Old School, Dore
FINISH	Hathersage village centre
PARKING	On road in Dore
PUBLIC TOILETS	In Hathersage
REFRESHMENTS	Two pubs (Devonshire Arms and Hare & Hounds) and a cafe in Dore. Plenty of choice in Hathersage
TRAINS & BUSES	Train and bus services 30, 98, 272 and M17

Route Directions

A Leave the Old School yard by the large gateway, turn left (Savage Lane), walk up to the T-junction, turn left, cross the road into Townhead Road and continue for about 700m. At the end of Townhead Road continue into Whitelow Lane. The road descends then climbs for about 1½km (1 mile) to meet Hathersage Road. At the junction, cross the to the public footpath sign and go through the gate onto moorland (Houndkirk Moor).

B The clear path climbs steadily for about 400m to a concrete marker post.

The path marked on OS maps goes straight ahead but is often very wet. The following route keeps to dryer ground and should result in less plant damage.

C Leave the marker post by the path that follows a line slightly to the left of the line by which you approached. Continue, looking back at the post occasionally to check that you are maintaining the same line. After about 200m look for a second concrete post, about 250m away, which is to the right of your walking line. Continue on the path, which now bears gently to the right, to pass close to the second concrete post. At this post, look ahead just below the skyline, to locate a public footpath sign. The path you are on leads direct to this sign, which is on the byway (Houndkirk Road).

D Cross the byway at the sign and continue ahead to follow a well defined track, rising higher onto the moor. Soon you will have views ahead to Carl Wark and Higger Tor. The path then starts to go downhill and, having first passed two single cairns, you reach two cairns close together at a junction of paths. Bear right at the first cairn and then take the path, immediately to the left of the second cairn, that leads down to a wide passing track (Duke's Drive).

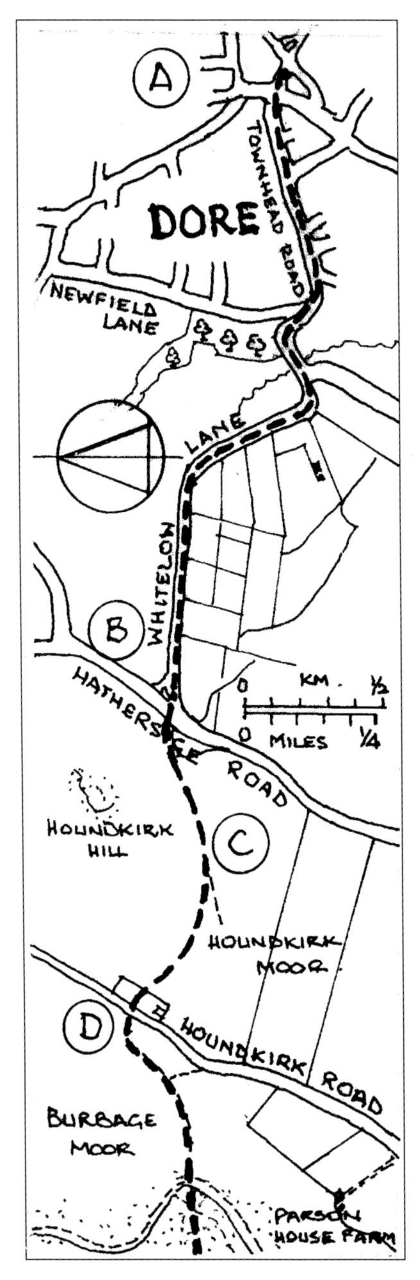

E Turn left here and after 80m turn right onto another signed path. This path goes downhill to an old packhorse bridge to the left of a bank of trees. **See Packhorse Bridge**.

PACKHORSE BRIDGE: We are following the line of the former Dore-Hathersage bridleway which crossed the Burbage Brook at this point. Burbage means a stream near a fortification, doubtless Carl Wark. The bridge is not far from two settlement sites on Longshaw and also smelting sites dating from the Iron Age (the four centuries BC).

Packhorse Bridge, Burbage

From here bear uphill to the right, to pass close to the right hand side of Carl Wark, the hill on your left. **See** both **Carl Wark** and **Higger Tor.**

CARL WARK : Carl Wark was traditionally thought to date from the Iron Age. It is an enormous rectangular hill-fort entered from the south-west at an altitude of 381m (1250ft) and covering nearly 0.8ha (2 acres). Its most impressive feature is a towering 45m (148ft) long western wall of gritstone blocks, found in a 1950 excavation to be bonded into turf. This prompted a Dark Ages date (400-600 AD), as contemporary Scottish forts use this Roman technique. The jury is still out. Both Celtic *cair* and Old English *weorc* mean fortification, but antiquarian S. O. Addy makes 'Carl' a Norse compliment to Odin!

F When you arrive at the crossing track between Carl Wark and Higger Tor, go directly across it on to a somewhat indistinct but initially wide path across the moorland. Looking ahead at this point, aim for a single.

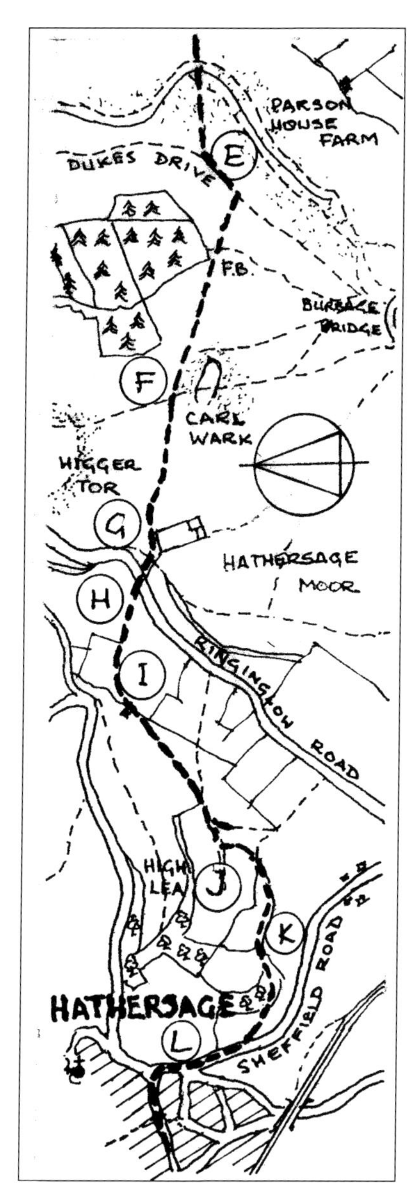

tree on the horizon in the near distance. Approaching this tree, walk to the right of a large walled enclosure

G Arriving at the tree you will see that in fact there is a group of small trees. This point provides a lovely view ahead up the valley towards Hathersage and Hope beyond. With a wall to your left, the path now goes steeply downhill to the left of these trees, through a gate and then down to meet the road. (Ringinglow Road).

HIGGER TOR: Looming above Carl Wark, at 434m (1424ft) Higger Tor is 53m *higher* than the nearby tor on which the hill-fort came to be built. Recorded as Higher Tor in 1809, it presumably got its name from this fact. Both tors are outliers from the main gritstone mass at Burbage Rocks. The footpath that you crossed actually ascends Higger Tor. Septuagenarians and above should think twice before attempting it from this direction.

H Go directly across the road and over a stile to walk downhill across Mitchells Fields. When you have crossed the fields, you will arrive at a crossing track at which you turn left. However, take a moment to walk a few metres to the right to read the sign on the award-winning barn conversion. Now return to the correct direction and walk along the track; a few metres after the entrance on your right to the farmyard, follow the footpath sign on your right.

I This proceeds through a small bank of trees to a stile. Cross this stile and bear diagonally right across the corner of the field to another stone stile. Cross this and continue diagonally to your left climbing across the field. This path brings you to an isolated hall.

J The footpath proceeds through the metal gate into the grounds of the hall, then down the long drive and out again through the far (powered) wooden gate. Go straight ahead with the wall on your right and then continue ahead when the access track to the hall veers to the left. The path goes downhill to a stile in a wall at the edge of a wood. **See Holloway.**

Winter walkers on Carl Wark

HOLLOWAY: Near the west end of the old Dore-Hathersage bridleway, the holloway from the wood below Scraperlow to the A6187 prompts a little history lesson. Hillside paths deepened over centuries of heavy use and the action of melting ice and fast-flowing water. Ancient trackways followed the most direct route possible. Indirect but easier links from Dore to the Fox House-Hathersage road authorized in 1781 followed the fringes of Blacka: another bridleway and from 1818 the Dore Turnpike.

K Cross the stile and walk forward with the wall on your left. Keep directly ahead on this path through the wood, with views across the valley on your left. The path goes downhill and arrives at a small gate.

Going through this gate you enter a sunken lane that continues downhill and in due course meets the main Hathersage to Sheffield road. At this point there is a bus stop for Sheffield a few metres to your left up the hill.

L Crossing the road (carefully) and turning right, you will arrive in Hathersage in 5 to 10 minutes. There is a bus stop in the middle of Hathersage by the post office and several pubs, coffee shops and a deli. **See Hathersage.**

The railway station is just off the B6001 road to Grindleford and about 600m from the village centre.

HATHERSAGE: Hathersage, called Hereseige in Domesday Book, may mean invaders edge (Barbara Buxton), but Kenneth Cameron plumps for Hafer s ridge . The first church was built in the early 1130s as tithing support for the new Launde Abbey, Leicestershire. Enlargement began in 1381 when a new nave was added and the old one became the north aisle. Hathersage Hall s fa ade of 1820 conceals much 17t h century work. Manufactures included millstones, wire and wire products (needles and various pins), textiles, buttons and malt.

Hathersage Church

GRINDLEFORD TO DORE

Why not enjoy a short train journey before heading back to Dore? The walk contrasts the woodland of Padley Gorge with the more open ground of Longshaw and Blacka.

DISTANCE	10km (6 miles)
MINIMUM TIME	3 hours
TERRAIN	Easy walking with one or two steepish sections
LANDSCAPE	Woodland and wide views over Burbage and Sheffield
START	Grindleford Station
FINISH	Old School, Dore
PUBLIC TOILETS	Fox House
REFRESHMENTS	Grindleford Station cafe, Longshaw Visitor Centre, Fox House, two pubs (Devonshire Arms and Hare & Hounds) and a cafe in Dore
TRAINS & BUSES	Train to Grindleford

This walk begins by taking the train from Dore & Totley Station to Grindleford.

Route Directions

A At the top of the path from the platform, turn left and cross back over the railway, noting Totley Tunnel entrance.

Totley Tunnel, Grindleford

Walking ahead, follow the rough road over the stream (Burbage Brook), past Padley Mill on your right. Shortly after this, turn right, following the signpost to Longshaw Estate via Padley Gorge. Climb up the rough road and enter the woods at a gate with a sign declaring that the Longshaw Visitor Centre is two miles. Continue ahead uphill through the woods of Padley Gorge on a well-defined stoned path (on your left you will see an old shelter with air vents). Shortly after this on your right, is a waterfall, which can be spectacular after wet weather.

In about 1200m (¾ mile) exit the woods at a gate and keep straight ahead. After a short distance you will see a wooden bridge on your right. Ignore this and continue ahead with the stream still on your right. After a further 400m, cross the next wooden bridge on your right and climb the stone path following it around a sharp right-hand bend at a small waterfall. Go through a kissing gate and keep straight on through the conifer wood.

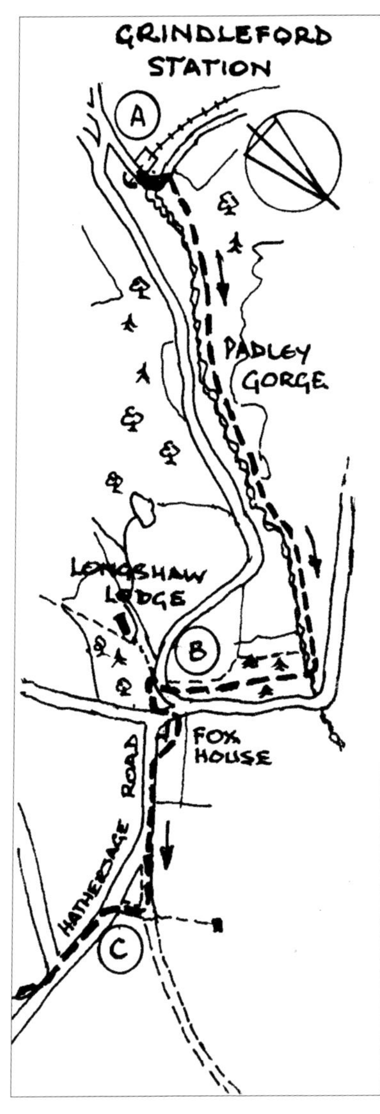

Go through a small gate to arrive at a road (Grindleford to Fox House).

B Turn right, cross the road and after 20m enter the drive to Longshaw Estate, with a lodge on the left. **See Longshaw Lodge.**

At this point you could divert to the National Trust cafe for refreshments. To do this, walk down the drive for about 200m and turn left to the cafe. Retrace your steps to the lodge afterwards.

LONGSHAW LODGE: Longshaw was built about 1827 as the Duke of Rutland's shooting lodge. A century later they sold Longshaw Lodge with 303ha (747 acres) of land for £13,000 to the recently formed Association for the Protection of Rural Scenery, who transferred it to the National Trust. Originally with its own chapel and plenty of room for servants and horses, the Lodge has been turned into private flats. The Meadow has hosted sheepdog trials since 1898.

Then immediately double back left at the lodge on a path signed Fox House Bus Stop. Keep straight on at the next junction of paths and climb up to a gate at the main road opposite the Fox House pub. **See Fox House.**

FOX HOUSE: The pub has an internal datestone of 1690, but veteran rambler G.H.B. Ward on the evidence of wills dated it to the mid-1770s. Extensions began with the Duke of Rutland s agent in the 1840s. In 1880 it was the Traveller s Rest, a beerhouse. Later it was named after a member of the Fox family of Callow above Hathersage, who supposedly built the original cottage. The rubble public bridleway (Houndkirk Road) up the road was part of the Sheffield & Buxton Turnpike.

Turn left. Then, as the pavement runs out, cross the road and go up a path diagonally to the right. This takes you round the left hand side of the pub buildings and leads to the pub car park. Leave by the car park entrance and turn left up the main road (Hathersage Road), taking care as there is no footpath. In about 300m, where the main road bends to the right, bear left up a rubble public bridleway which is the end of the Houndkirk Road. Just before a gate at the farm entrance turn right, going down the drive back to the main road.

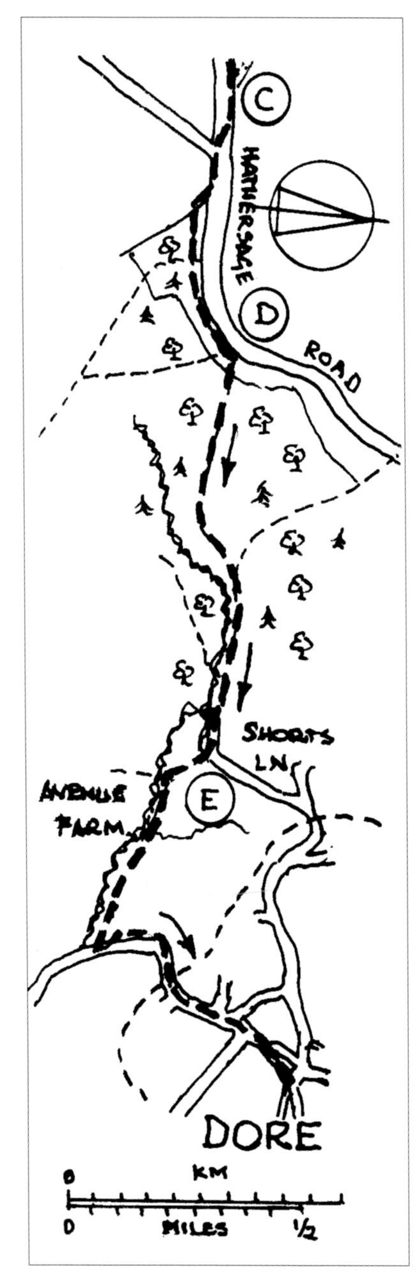

C Turn left, cross the road and follow the footpath over the brow of the hill. Cross over a joining side road, continue down the main road for a short distance and then turn right into a small car park. **See Stony Ridge.**

STONY RIDGE: The site of the Stony Ridge tollbar is marked with a commemorative stone on the opposite side of the main road. The only tollbar on the Dore Turnpike Road, it opened in 1816 and closed in 1884. It resembled a single-storey Scottish cottage. The road itself was built by Dore labourers mainly at the expense of the Duke of Devonshire. Its purpose was to by-pass the more hilly and exposed Ringinglow and Houndkirk roads between Banner Cross Hall and Fox House, and it seems to have been popular with local people.

Turn left through a gap in the wall and keep straight on the footpath as it descends gently through the woods to a gate. Continue down the path keeping to the left and parallel to the main road, ignoring any tracks to the right, until you reach a junction of paths with a 'Welcome to Blacka Moor' sign.

Stony Ridge Tollbar site

D Turn right here and continue downhill. At the next junction of paths, where extensive views of Sheffield open up, keep straight on down a steep hill. At a gate keep straight on once more and descend rapidly taking care on the often loose surface. After about 400m keep straight on at a bridleway sign for Shorts Lane, ignoring the signpost to

Devil's Elbow Gate to your left. The track continues ahead and soon leaves the Blacka Moor Reserve. Continue ahead on the track.

E Just after a sharp left bend as a tarmac road begins (Shorts Lane), turn right at a public footpath sign and descend a field with a wire fence on your left. At the bottom, turn left without crossing the stream and after a short distance go through a gated gap stile in the wall.

Keep to the right hand edge when crossing the next field, with the stream on your right, then go through a gated stile and continue ahead along a metalled drive to the road (Old Hay Lane).

Turn left, then immediately left again over a stone stile and ascend the right hand edge of a field. Cross over a stile, rejoin the road and keep straight along the road to the centre of the village.

Gritstone and pines above Burbage Brook

LONGSHAW, OAK'S WOOD AND PADLEY

Without being too energetic, this walk provides a varied mix of scenery including a little used stretch through Oak's and Yarncliff Woods. Tea and a sticky bun await at Longshaw!

DISTANCE	7¾km (4¾ miles)
MINIMUM TIME	2½ hours
TERRAIN	Good paths throughout
LANDSCAPE	Open moorland and woodland
START/FINISH	Woodcroft Car Park, Longshaw
PARKING	Woodcroft Car Park, Longshaw
PUBLIC TOILETS	Longshaw, visitor centre, none on route
REFRESHMENTS	Longshaw visitor centre, Grouse Inn and Fox House (slightly off route)
TRAINS & BUSES	Services 65, 214, 240 and 272

Route Directions

A Starting in the upper level of the car park and facing the vehicle entrance, walk diagonally to your right to reach a gap in the wall. Pass through this and follow the path for about 80m to the right to reach a gate in another wall. Pass through this and turn right to proceed with the wall and wood on your right. After about 300m and where the trees on your right finish, the track joins a wider path. Bear left to follow the signpost direction to Wooden Pole Car Park. **See Longshaw Estate South: Turnpikes.**

After a further 500m and where the track divides, bear to the right towards the edge of a band of trees. The Wooden Pole can be seen high to the left. **See Wooden Pole**. Continue on this path to reach the drive to the alternative car park. Cross over this and go through a gate. Cross the busy road (A625) to the white gate diagonally opposite.

LONGSHAW ESTATE SOUTH: TURNPIKES: As you turn left towards Wooden Pole, you are on the Hathersage branch of the Greenhill Moor Turnpike. Authorized in 1781, this ran from the original Chesterfield Turnpike at Dyche Lane to Calver along the line of today s B6054 and A625. When after 500m the track divides you keep on the old turnpike, noting the branch to the left. This was a later addition to avoid an extremely sharp turn for Holmesfield traffic which you can picture as you reach the main road.

B Go through this gate and enter White Edge Moor. Continue ahead through woodland for about 250m to reach another gate. Pass through this and continue on the path as it bears to the right. Continue on the well-trodden path as it passes through a copse of trees and then becomes a sunken path.

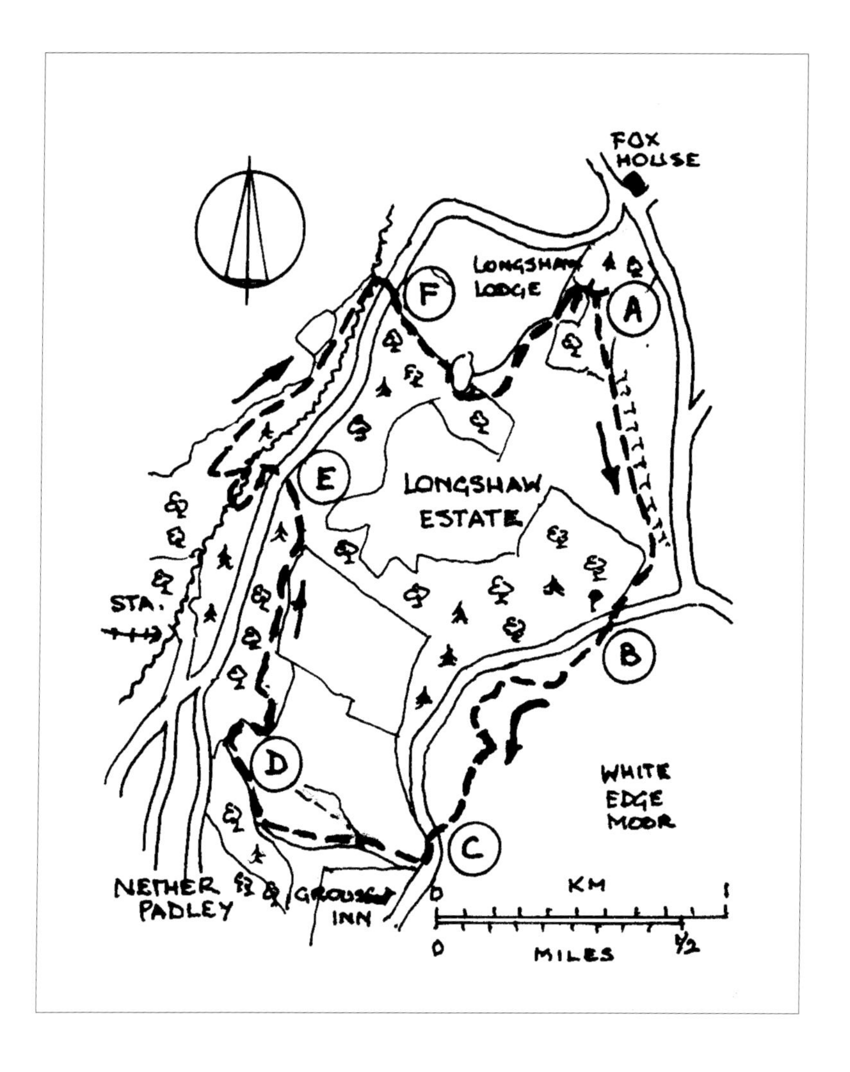

WOODEN POLE: The original wooden pole was an ancient bridleway guidepole said to have marked the track from Dronfield to Tideswell. When Mafeking Day was celebrated during the Boer W ar the Afrikaaners siege of this town was lifted on 17 May 1900 it becam e a flagstaff. At its foot is a boundary stone marked T 1778 , probably referring to Totley, and TW , thought to be Thomas Willoughby, otherwise Lord Middleton, lord of the manor of Totley.

The path then comes into the open, with views ahead and to the right. White Edge Lodge comes into view to the left. Here the path veers to the right; you ignore the path to your left leading up to the Lodge. Follow the path downhill to the road (A625).

C Cross the road and, ignoring the footpath sign to Longshaw, turn left and walk for about 100m beside the road to a wooden gate and footpath sign on the right, just before a right hand bend in the road. At this point the Grouse Inn is just a little further along the road. Go through the gate and follow the track bearing left towards a gate and National Trust sign Jubilee. **See Jubilee Area.**

JUBILEE AREA: Jubilee is the name of this part of the Longshaw Estate. It includes Tumbling Hill, from which there are fine views. Traditionally bonfires were lit here to celebrate the jubilees of kings and queens. A recent one was the Silver Jubilee of Elizabeth II in June 1977. Yarncliff Quarry, a former millstone quarry belonging to the Eyre family, is about 1 km north of Tumbling Hill.

Do not go through this gate but continue past it, keeping the wall on your immediate left. After passing through the second crossing wall, take the path half right leading across the middle of the field. Noting the views of Hathersage ahead, follow the path as it descends across the field towards a gate in a wall and a bank of trees.

D Go through the gate and immediately turn right, with another wall now on your left. Keep this wall on your left and walk steeply down to cross a stream. If this descent looks particularly muddy, you could continue to your right for a few more paces and find an easier crossing. Once across, follow the path to the left to arrive at another stream. After crossing this one, ignore the path to your immediate left and follow the path ahead as it climbs gently, with a wood (Oak's Wood) on your left.

When this path approaches a crossing wall, turn left onto a broader path and continue with the wall now on your right. The path leads past a gate to steps over a wall and then turns right to enter woodland. Keep ahead, ignoring a path on the left going downhill. Note the views of Grindleford Station down to your left. The path climbs a little, arrives at a wall on your right and then re-enters the wood (Yarncliff Wood). Soon there is a junction of paths. The main path turns up to the right but you take the left, smaller, one leading gently down through the trees. Keep ahead on this path for about 300m, ignoring others to your right, until it arrives at the road (B6521). Yarncliff Quarry is nearby.

Jubilee, Longshaw Estate

E Cross the road and turn left, walking down for about 30m to a National Trust sign Padley Gorge on your right. **See Padley Gorge.** Follow this sign through the wall, turn left and follow the path down, with the brook (Burbage Brook) below to your right. At a fork of paths go straight ahead, ignoring others to the left and the right, and continue down for about 150m to reach stone steps on the path.

Longshaw pines in winter

50m after these, take the path to your right and descend more steps to reach the wooden footbridge over the brook.

PADLEY GORGE: Padley Gorge is ancient woodland. In medieval times it was on the edge of the High Peak Forest, a vast area interspersed with commons and waste where deer were hunted. Domestic stockbreeding increased and in the 17th century the High Peak was legally disafforested, so the deer disappeared. Padley Gorge escaped the clearances and the National Trust now manages it as a major Site of Special Scientific Interest. If you are a twitcher you may spot wood warblers or pied flycatchers here.

Cross this, climb steeply up the bank and, at a stone bench, follow the path as it bends sharply left to climb more steps to join the main path. Turn right here and follow the main path uphill, with the brook now down on the right, for about 800m. Ignore any alternative paths to your right. Pass through a gate almost at the end of the woodland, and as the path leaves the woodland, continue beside the brook until a footbridge is reached on the right. Cross this and follow the path up to a gate. **See Hollowgate.**

HOLLOWGATE: On exiting Padley Gorge you soon see Hollowgate, a deep track coming down at half left with a sharp left turn above. (There s a much better view from the main road on your right.) David Hey describes this as a quarry road from Millstone Edge, crossing Burbage Brook and then forking towards Fox House and Sheffield and towards Big Moor and Chesterfield. Probably an existing track, it was artificially deepened. How the millstones and other quarry products were transported is uncertain but horse-drawn sledges may have been the means.

F Go through this gate and cross the road (B 6521) diagonally right to a footpath sign beside a gate. Go through this and follow the main path through trees, with a fence on your left, and eventually reach a lake. Immediately after the lake, the path bends to the left and passes through a gate to continue between rhododendrons. The next gate takes you onto a grassed area, with views of Carl Wark ahead.

A further gate takes you into another area of rhododendrons, with a ha-ha feature on the right, and soon to a junction of paths in a shaded area under trees next to a wall. Take the first left path here to pass in front of Longshaw Lodge, on your right, to the Visitor Centre. **See Longshaw Lodge.** Here turn left and, after 20m, turn right to follow the sign to the Estate Office. At a junction of paths take the left path, signposted to Woodcroft car park.

LONGSHAW LODGE: Longshaw was built about 1827 as the Rutlands shooting lodge. A century later they sold Longshaw Lodge with 303ha (747 acres) of land for £13,000 to the recently formed Association for the Protection of Rural Scenery, who transferred it to the National Trust. Originally with its own chapel and plenty of room for servants and horses, the Lodge has been turned into private flats. The Meadow has hosted sheepdog trials since 1898.

Longshaw Lodge

NORTH LEES AND STANAGE EDGE

Combining the wonderful views from Stanage Edge and the historical connections of North Lees and Hathersage, this walk can easily be done from Dore using either bus or train.

DISTANCE	10km (6¼ miles)
MINIMUM TIME	3½ hours
TERRAIN	Grass paths, tracks and roads. The ascent past North Lees Hall to Stanage Edge should be taken steadily
LANDSCAPE	A mix of farm, wood and moorland, with rewarding views from Stanage Edge
START/FINISH	The Outside shop on Main Road in Hathersage
PARKING	The Oddfellows Road public car park in Hathersage
PUBLIC TOILETS	In Hathersage and at the foot of Stanage Edge
REFRESHMENTS	Plenty of choice in Hathersage but none on route
TRAINS & BUSES	Train and bus services 65, 214, 240, 272 and 284

Route Directions

From the bottom right hand corner of the car park take the footpath which leads to the main road close to the Outside shop.

A From the Outside shop, cross the road, turn right and continue uphill for about 150m and turn left at the public footpath sign into Baulk Lane. After 150m, turn right at the public footpath sign on an uphill path with a wall on the right. Continue, through a pair of gates, and enter the churchyard, now on the tarmac path with a wall on the left. You pass Little John's grave on the right before reaching the lych gate. **See Little John's Grave**.

B Here turn left and continue for 60m to reach the stile ahead. Take the track round to the right and, after about 50m, turn left down steps down to a small stream. Cross this and then continue ahead, keeping to the lower side of the field. After 200m, and where the paths divide, bear diagonally right uphill towards a marker post. Continue in the same line towards thorn bushes where the path bears left. Soon take the stile and continue ahead, ignoring a large gate on the left, through the fields towards farm buildings.

LITTLE JOHN S GRAVE: If we think that Robin Hood and Little John were characters of fiction, this 3.5m grave must give us pause. And what about Robin Hood s Cave on Stanage Edge and Little John s Well on Longshaw? Certainly the remains of a very tall man were found when the grave was opened in 1784. The problem is that Robin and his men have no place in early 13th century records. Yet as Barbara Buxton, Hathersage s historian, points out, a century later robber bands led by minor gentry indeed roamed Derbyshire. James Coterel s gang was in league with the Bradburnes of Hulland, whose retainers included a certain John the Little . Was this our man?

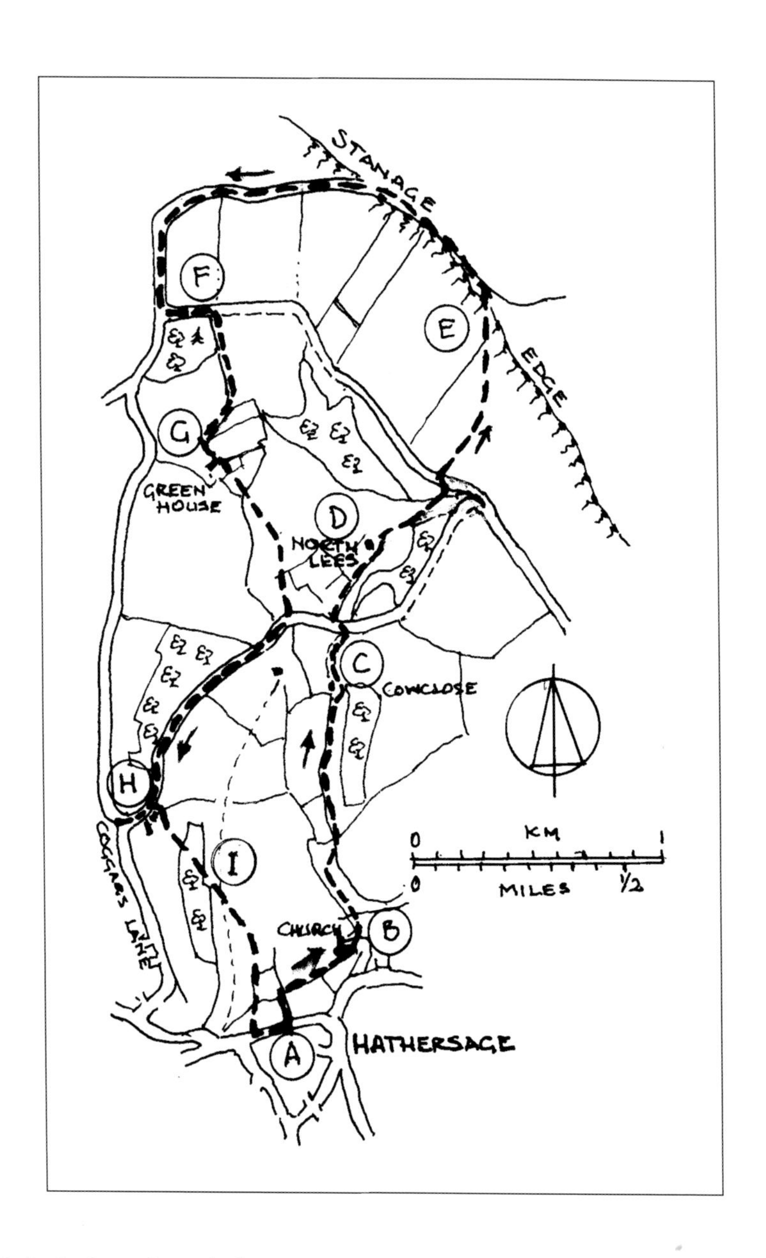

C At the farm, the path skirts round the right hand side of the stone buildings before exiting through a wooden gate in a fence. Do not take the drive from the farm but continue at the lower side of the field ahead. The path curves to the right before entering woodland and reaching a stile with a flight of steps down to the road. Turn left, pass the entrance to North Lees

Campsite and then, after about 100m, turn right into the tarmac drive up to North Lees Hall. **See North Lees Hall.**

At the time of writing the plaques, at each side of this entrance to indicate the Hall, had been removed.

NORTH LEES HALL: We first hear of North Lees Hall in the 16th century. The tower at the back has a spiral staircase and Perpendicular (to 1530) doorcases; the rest is 1594 or later. In 1588 its Catholic lessor Richard Fenton shared in the troubles of his Fitzherbert relations. A century later James II relaxed anti-Catholic laws and a chapel was built nearby; a Protestant mob promptly demolished it. For a short time one of the local Eyre families giving their name to Charlotte Bront° s heroine liv ed here.

D At the Hall, go ahead between walls and then, after about 100m, turn sharp right on to a track that becomes a grass path leading towards a fir wood.

Wall building, Hathersage

Cross a stile and continue ahead through the woodland, now between wire fences. At the end of the left hand fence, turn left uphill on a stone paved path heading to a toilet building. About 20m before reaching this, bear right to a gate, cross the road and continue ahead up a grass path towards woodland. Before reaching this, a more used path from the car park joins from the left. Continue on this roughly paved path through the woodland (Stanage Plantation) and right up to the top of the escarpment (Stanage Edge).

E Here turn left on to a path that runs along the Edge for about 200m to a square metal post, marked *Sheffield Country Walk,* where you should bear left and follow the stony bridleway (Long Causeway) down for about 1½km (1 mile). **See Long Causeway.** About 200m after passing a copse of mixed trees on the left, this reaches a parking area at a road corner. Turn left and walk down for 200m to reach a cattle grid.

LONG CAUSEWAY: There has been a lot of speculation about the Long Causeway. Some think it was part of a Roman road from Brough near Bradwell via Stanage Edge to Templeborough. Others consider it medieval, placing the line of the Roman road further north by Stanedge Lodge. Salters from Cheshire may have come this way to Sheffield there is a Saltergate Lane nearby in Bamford and perhaps it w as a route for pack animals carrying lead from the Peak to Bawtry and transhipment for London.

F About 15m past this, turn right to take the path with a wall on the right. After about 200m, take the stile in the wall into the signposted Longshaw Estate and turn left taking the path with the wall now on your left. Follow this down, past a gateway, the wall eventually giving way to a wire fence. The path continues to drop until it reaches a gate leading into a drive with a house (Green's House) ahead. **See Green's House.**

G Here turn left and head for the wide gate. Immediately past this, turn right between wire fences and then continue ahead through fields before entering a wood. Continue ahead again, with a small stream on your right, to reach a wooden bridge over a larger stream (Hood Brook) coming down from the left.

GREEN S HOUSE: About 350m east of Green s House, in a wood and just north of the footpath to Hook s Car, is the dam of a former lead mill. By the 1760s it was a paper mill and it retained this function for a century. Water power was needed for pulping the rags, and the site high up the valley offered spring water of maximum purity. In 1857 the mill was worked by Charles Marsden who manufactured coarse brown wrapping paper.

Turn right after the bridge and continue through fields to reach a road (Birley Lane). At the road, turn right, cross the bridge and then take the road uphill for about 1km to reach farm buildings on the left.

Stile near North Lees Hall

A short detour here will take you to an interesting historic location. Continue along the road and, after about 150m, you will reach the junction with Coggers Lane. Ahead of you is a stone pillar bearing a plaque marking the location of Hathersage's first school, something that is also referred to as the school in the village of Morton in Charlotte Brontë's *Jane Eyre*. **See Hathersage & Brontë Connections.**

From here you also get an excellent view up the Hope Valley towards Mam Tor. Retrace your steps along Birley Lane to the farm.

H Before the first building (or, if you have taken the detour, just past the farm buildings), take the stile beside the wide metal gate and turn left to another gate some 25m away. Follow the track that swings sharp right and then, after about 75m, take the stile on the left. Head for a nearby concrete post and then bear half right down the field, keeping close to the hedge on the right. About 100m before the field end, bear left downhill to a stile in the lower right hand corner of the field under trees. The path now heads down through woodland (Cliff Wood), over another stile and continues in the same general direction past marker posts.

I The path crosses the tarmac drive and, still on the same line, eventually reaches a concrete bridge over the brook. Turn right here and then follow the path, keeping close to the brook all the way, through fields until it reaches houses. Bear right past the back gardens of these and then soon reach the main road (Main Road), opposite the Outside shop.

HATHERSAGE & BRONT¸ CONNECTI ONS: Hathersage Old Vicarage experienced interesting times around 1845. Charlotte Bront° spent three w eeks here visiting her friend Ellen Nussey. Ellen s brother the Rev Henry proposed to her; Charlotte turned him down. Then a wealthier lady said Yes! and Henry extended the vicarage to celebrate, adding the westernmost bay to the front. Jane Eyre was published two years later. Hathersage is thought to be Morton , North Lees Hall (see above) Thornfield Hall , and Moorseats Moor House . But these locations are hotly contested by Bront° fans in W est Yorkshire.

MOORHALL, UNTHANK & CARTLEDGE

Starting from Millthorpe, this delightful walk provides some different views of the Cordwell Valley and passes three fine halls.

DISTANCE	7¾km (4¾ miles)
MINIMUM TIME	2½ hours
TERRAIN	Easy going but some some steady climbs
LANDSCAPE	Farmland and woodland
START/FINISH	Millthorpe, near Holmesfield
PARKING	Lay-by on Millthorpe Lane near the garden centre
PUBLIC TOILETS	None on route
REFRESHMENTS	Royal Oak, Millthorpe
TRAINS & BUSES	Services 14, 89 and 293

MILLTHORPE: Given its name, Millthorpe must be an early industrial site, but let s be literary for once. A short distance along Cordwell Lane, towards Owler Bar, is the house of Edward Carpenter (1844-1929). A former curate and university lecturer, soon rebelling against Victorian conventions, he settled here in 1883, tried to get back to nature and became known for his advanced writings on sex and William Morris-style socialism. He had lived briefly at Totley and Lower Bradway and later moved to Guildford.

Route Directions

A From the car park go downhill to the crossroads and then take Mill Lane opposite down to the ford. Cross the ford and continue ahead for approximately 200m to a stone stile on the right in a wall marked 'Mill Farm'. Cross the stile, follow the left side of the first field then go diagonally right in the second, heading to the footbridge. Cross this, climb two stiles then follow the left side of the field up to a gateway. Keep to the right of the next field for about 100m and then head half left towards a gap in the trees. Cross the stream and then head half left up the bank to reach the lane (Johnnygate Lane) opposite Barlow Woodseats Hall. **See Barlow Woodseats Hall.**

B Turn right and follow the lane up through the wood (Hollin Wood). After nearly 1½km (1 mile), reach the road at Moorhall. Turn right uphill for about 70m and then turn right down the drive past Moor Green Farm. About 30m before the gateway into Moorhall Farm, take the stile on your left and pass the barn on your right. Take the stile in the wall to the left of the yard gate and head for a marker post about 150m into the middle of this field. Continue past this to a gap in the trees to cross a small stream. Continue on this line to a gate into a wood (Meekfield Wood).

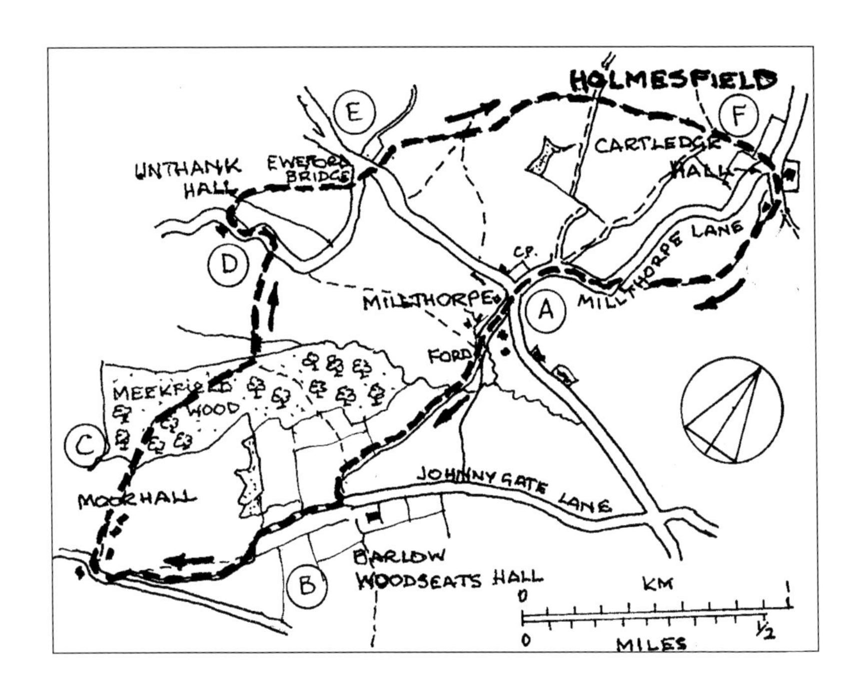

Barlow Woodseats Hall

BARLOW WOODSEATS HALL: The name Woodseats indicates a post-Conquest settlement, in a woodland clearing, on the fringe of an older one from Anglo-Saxon times. The Mower family held the manor as early as the 14th century. 300 years later they had grown rich from lead smelting and in 1624 Arthur Mower re-built and enlarged Barlow Woodseats in sandstone with ashlar dressings. Parts of the present building may be earlier. The east range and one of the barns contain several crucks.

C When the path divides, bear left down to cross the stream and then follow the path for about 700m through the wood. Where another path joins from the right, turn left through the stile into a field and head for a gateway ahead. Continue, with the hedge on your right, to a squeeze stile into the next field where you keep the hedge on your left to reach another stile to the right of the cottage ahead. Turn left at the lane (Unthank Lane) and continue uphill until reaching Unthank Hall. **See Unthank Hall.**

UNTHANK HALL: The name of this remote place is probably self-explanatory it w as a thankless task to work it though it might just mean a squatter s settlement. Unthank Hall goes back to the 16th century and is highly regarded by architectural historians as it is remarkably unadorned and unaltered. The reason for this may well be that for three centuries up to 1985 it was not farmed by the owners but let to the same family, the Lowes.

D Take the path opposite the Hall and, following the wall on your right, turn right where the wall turns right and go to the gateway ahead. Keeping to the right, move to the gap at the end of this field before heading diagonally left down the slope, then over the stile to the gate. Turn left towards the bridge (Eweford Bridge, over Millthorpe Brook) then right at the T–junction. After 75m on the road, search for the (possibly obscured) signpost on the left and go up the stone steps and over the stile.

Cartledge Hall

E Continue uphill with the hedge on your left for 200m, then bear diagonally right across the field to a gap in the hedge. Continue diagonally uphill to the top corner of the field, cross the stile and the footbridge. Cross the next field, diagonally to the left, up to the stile halfway along the top boundary wall. Continue uphill for about 100m then bear slightly right to cross the stile. Walk along the bottom of the next field and continue across the following field to the stile.

Cross the sunken path and go through the gate ahead. Continue through three fields. In the third field, head to the stile visible in the hedge ahead and slightly to the left. Cross the centre of the next field, go through the gate ahead, across the foot bridge and then bear left uphill. Join a lane, between hedges, that leads to Millthorpe Lane. Turn left and after a short distance, where the road bends to the left, turn right (Cartledge Lane). **See Cartledge Hall.**

CARTLEDGE HALL: This impressive hall is mainly a 1620s rebuild by Thomas Burton, brother of Michael of Holmesfield Hall, with some 16th century remains and 19th century additions (but see Cartledge Grange below). Lead smelting had brought the Burtons immense wealth. It later saw many owners and tenants, including the writer Robert Murray Gilchrist. In the mid-20th century it fell into disrepair. Basil Doncaster and his son Richard restored it. It contains plasterwork from the former Greenhill Hall and a carved fireplace from Attercliffe Hall.

F Continue ahead to pass the old halls on the left (Cartledge Hall and Cartledge Grange). **See Cartledge Grange.** After 100m, at the point where the tarmac road ends, bear right to pass Cartledge Cottage on the right and enter the drive to Cartledge Hall Farm (do not go straight ahead down the signed public bridleway).

CARTLEDGE GRANGE: Cartledge Grange came into the hands of John Wolstenholme of Horsleygate Hall and in 1556 through his heiress Alice it passed to Thomas Burton senior. It is no surprise that its history is intertwined with that of Cartledge Hall. Perhaps it was itself an earlier Cartledge Hall. (One theory has it that the later Cartledge Hall began in about 1585 as a dower house for Alice in her widowhood.) The Grange was re-built by descendants of Thomas and Alice.

Continue through the farmyard and then, bearing slightly right, down a lane for 200m to a stile to the right of a pair of gates. In the field ahead, keep left to a stile at the bottom corner leading into a private garden, through which is a public footpath leading to a driveway to Millthorpe Lane. Here turn left and follow the road down to the bottom to return to the start point.

CALVER, CURBAR GAP AND BASLOW

This walk will take you to three typical Peak District villages, each with its own slice of history, and then allow you to take advantage of the views from Baslow Edge

DISTANCE	8km (5 miles)
MINIMUM TIME	3 hours
TERRAIN	Good paths, some steep sections, up and down
LANDSCAPE	Riverside, woodland and an Edge with good views
START/FINISH	By the Bridge Inn, Calver (A623)
PARKING	Car park in front of Calver Primary School
PUBLIC TOILETS	None on route
REFRESHMENTS	Tea rooms and pubs in Calver and Baslow
TRAINS & BUSES	Bus services 214 and 240

Route Directions

A From the car park by the primary school, walk along the minor road in front of the Bridge Inn and, with the church on your right, cross the River Derwent via the footbridge beside the old bridge, with Calver Mill on your right. Take the subway under Baslow Road (A623), walk along the path with the river on your left and houses on your right and cross over the little bridge.

Keep straight ahead across the field with the river on your left. After about 500m go through squeeze stones in a stone wall, continue on with the river now running further away to the left and then go through old gateposts beside steps in the wall. Passing fine oak trees on your right, go through a wooden gate. After passing through more squeeze stones in a wall cross the field diagonally to the right to reach the wooden gates. Look high up to your right and see the E and R letters, formed by commemorative trees, on the distant slope.

B Arriving at the gates, turn left along the road and in 500m you reach Bubnell village. **See Bubnell**.

Walk straight on along the pavement as the river re-appears to your left with the houses of Baslow on the far bank. You will have a fine view of the weir, goyts and machinery of Baslow Mill.

The Toll House, Baslow

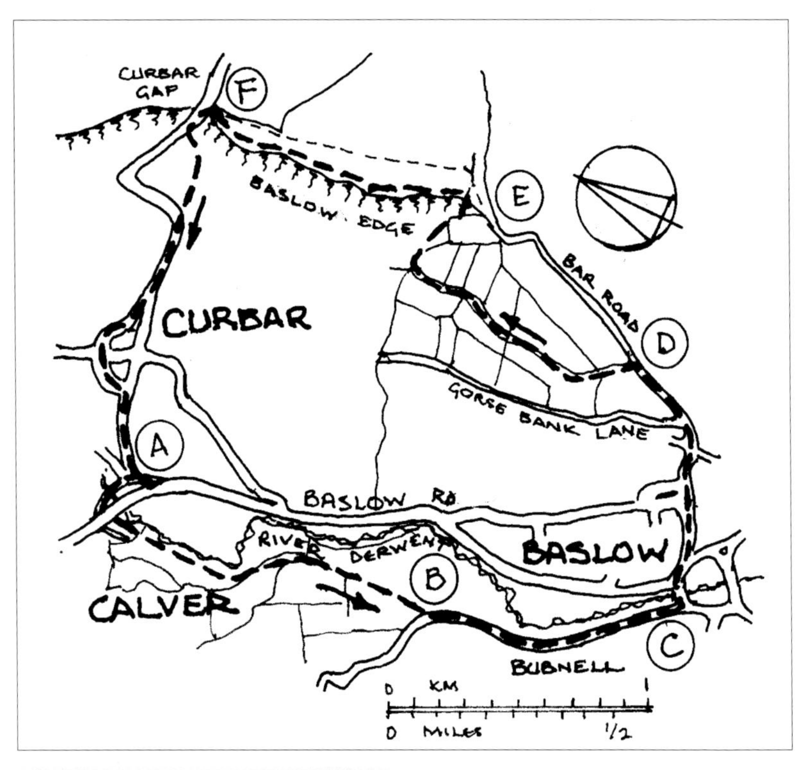

BUBNELL: Bubnell is said to mean Bubba s hill . The Hall is a good 17th century building with mullioned and transomed windows. It is interesting because the two wings projecting at the front look dramatically different: the windows of the east one are enormous. Up to the early 19th century, Bubnell was important for framework knitting, making hosiery. The mill opposite was a corn mill with bakehouse attached. The bridge dates from 1609.

C Turn left across the old river bridge. At the far end of the bridge is the toll collector's stone hut opposite Tollbar Cottage. **See Baslow.**

Turning right, cross the busy A623. Passing Baslow Church look for Victoria's name, commemorating her jubilee, on the clock, then take the left fork at the roundabout into School Lane. Walk past the Wesleyan Methodist Sunday School. After passing the Spar supermarket, fork left into Bar Road at the 'No through road' sign and the seat under the tree. Walk on up the hill. At the 'No vehicles' sign the road becomes rough with a square footpath sign on the right. Just before the road bends sharply right, turn left following a footpath sign beside a gate.

BASLOW: Baslow, Bassa s burial mound , has much early history: a bar , an ancient cross, medieval lead boles and a cloth fulling mill. The original Chesterfield Turnpike came down Bar Road from Bar Brook, continuing via Hassop and Great Longstone to Hernstone Lane Head (rival claims about where that was). But the tiny reputed tollhouse by the bridge is more likely a watchman s hut. Hydro Close at Over End commemorates the Baslow Hydropathic Establishment, flourishing in the 1880s-1920s, since demolished.

D As you continue, overlooking the valley to the left, you can again see the E and R on the hill. After 150m go through a wooden gate and walk on with the wall and several seats on your right for about 400m. Climb the steps over a wall and join a track curving up to the right and round between walls. Keep straight on beside the left hand wall to a stile by an iron six-bar gate.

Once over the stile, take the grassy track that forks up to the right towards the Edge. After only 30m turn right and walk on up the gravelled path between massive stones. The track bears right and soon there are distant views of Chatsworth House and the Emperor Fountain. Shortly, the track turns left through the quarry to arrive at an old stone track (Bar Road). Turn left and reach a seat from where you can see Wellington's Monument close by on your left and many distant features down the valley. Continue uphill for a few more metres to the point where a broad path comes into view on your left. From here you will have a good view of the Eagle Stone.

E You have a choice here. Either you follow the broad path to the left past the Eagle Stone, the path taking you directly across the Edge to reach Curbar Gap. Alternatively, turn sharply to the left and back on yourself to walk right to the edge of Baslow Edge. The path then bears right to take you along the Edge itself. This path is less distinct and involves a little undulation across the outcrop of rocks.

After about 20 minutes you will arrive at a viewpoint on your left. The track then takes you away from the edge and shortly arrives at the road at Curbar Gap.

The Eagle Stone

F Passing through the gate, turn left downhill along a path which runs alongside the road and in 150m turn left through a wooden gate following a footpath sign beside the Curbar Gap National Trust (NT) sign.

Stile at Curbar Gap

Soon the path passes through a wall under a sycamore tree, then down a flight of stone steps. Go down the hill, through another squeeze gate, then a

wooden gate beside another NT sign.
See Curbar.

CURBAR: Curbar s name first occurs as Cordeburg, Corda s fortified place . Like Baslow, Curbar has a Bar Road not as in Curbar it s a Celtic word meaning a hillcrest but in Derbyshire it means a steep bridleway. This became an 18th century turnpike road from Bar Brook through Curbar Gap and the walk descends its steepest part before it was by-passed by Clodhall Lane. Near this path are the Cundy Graves, with others in the village below the Wesley Reform chapel; the plague afflicted Curbar in 1632. Note also the circular lock-up.

Follow the path down to the road, turn left here and after 250m turn right into The Green, the first road on the right. Follow this road until you arrive at a crossing road. Here you will see an ancient well complex at the crossroads.

The Wells, Curbar

Go straight across at this junction and follow the road until it meets another crossing road, with the pinfold directly opposite. At the pinfold turn right and walk down the hill towards Calver Mill, turning left at the bottom to the car park by the primary school.

Bell heather over gritstone

FROGGATT, CURBAR AND WHITE EDGES

Ideal for a bright day with good visibility, this walk covers three Edges that characterise the northern part of the Derwent Valley. Will clear the head after a night out!

DISTANCE	8km (5 miles)
MINIMUM TIME	2½ hours
TERRAIN	Good paths with a couple of gentle climbs
LANDSCAPE	Panoramic views over moorland and dales
START/FINISH	Haywood Car Park, on A625 (Fox House to Froggatt and Calver)
PARKING	In car park
PUBLIC TOILETS	None on route
REFRESHMENTS	The Grouse Inn
TRAINS & BUSES	Not served direct by bus. Services 65, 214 and 240 go to the Maynard Arms, Nether Padley. Starting and finishing here adds 2km (1½ miles) to the total distance

Route Directions

The initial directions are included to enable bus users to get from the Maynard Arms to Haywood Car Park.

Alight at the Maynard Arms, continue for 50m downhill. Soon after the pavement ends, turn left up a footpath signed 'To Froggatt Edge road via Tedgness' (initially it may be overgrown but is manageable). Reaching the cul-de-sac, turn left then resume on the footpath immediately right. At the next road (Tedgness Road), turn left and two footpath signs appear on the right. Take the first path, sharp right, signed 'Haywood Car Park and Froggatt Edge'. Soon go through a gate and enter Haywood (NT sign). After 450m at a junction of paths, keep straight on, passing old quarries on the left. Go through the exit gate and immediately turn left uphill to the car park.

Stepping Stones, Hay Wood

A Walk south downhill out of the car park, bear left at a junction of paths, cross over a stream and then walk up to the road.

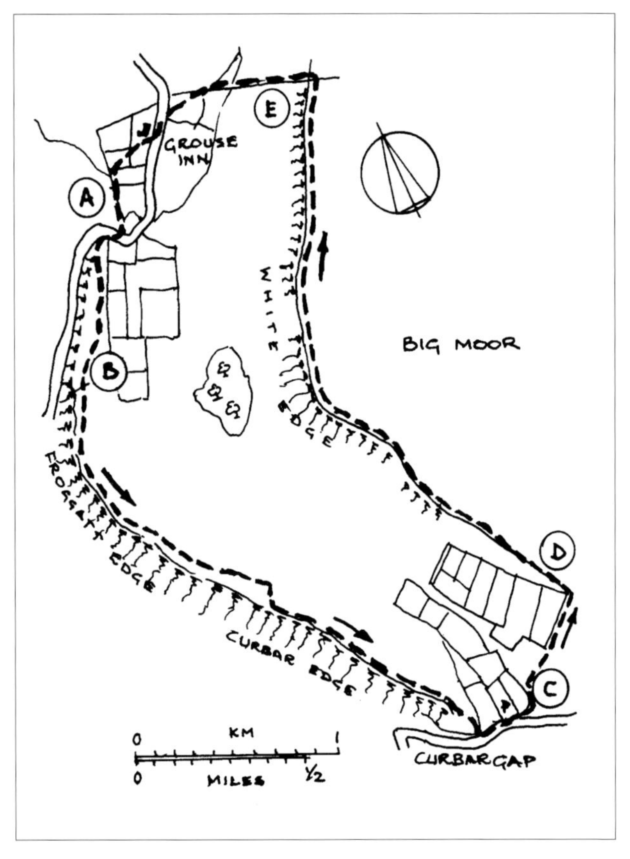

Turn right, cross the road and, after 30m, pass through the gate on your left. Continue up the wide track with a wall on your right, with views over the Derwent Valley, and after passing through a birch wood reach another gate after about 750m. **See Views from the Edges.**

B Continue ahead along Froggatt and Curbar Edges, noting the small stone circle on the left after 200m. Keep to the main path, ignoring a footpath sign on your right as the path veers to the left slightly uphill. A little further on the path divides into two, with the left hand route offering a gentle uphill track and the straight ahead route being a bit of a scramble. Both routes meet again after 200m.

VIEWS FROM THE EDGES: The views dramatically change as you walk on. Looking NW from Froggatt Edge, for example, on a clear day you can see the Kinder Scout plateau, 22‰km (14 miles) away, dwarfing Back Tor and Lose Hill in front of it. From Curbar Edge you can enjoy a closer prospect: look south to Edensor and the Chatsworth estate, WSW to the cloughs of Longstone beyond Calver, and west to Middleton Dale, while NW is Sir William Hill with its familiar mast.

After this, the main track is a little way from the edge but there is an alternative less well-marked path

much closer to the edge.
See Formation of the Edges.

FORMATION OF THE EDGES: As you stand on Curbar Edge or Froggatt Edge and look westwards, you are looking into the space once occupied by an extension of the rocks under your feet. They once rose ahead of you and over the hills on the skyline. In the recent geological past the incision of the River Derwent and its tributaries has created the valley side on which you are standing. Any rock exposure near you will be composed of grains of sand hence sandstones. When these grains are quite large (almost small pebbles), they are known as gritstones. Sandstones are more resistant to weathering and erosion than the shale beds that lie between them. Walking up from the valley floor on the eastern side of the Derwent is like walking up a large staircase within which each tread is the surface expression of another sandstone layer within the rock sequence.

This brings you near to the interesting rock formations and provides exceptional views over Eyam, Carver and Curbar. Eventually the track starts to descend and reaches a gate. Pass through this and take the left hand path with a wall on your left hand side. This leads into a picnic area and then crosses a small embankment into the Curbar Gap car park.

C Turn left out of the vehicle entrance to the car park and go through the gate to enter the Eastern Moors Estate. Continue ahead on a wide track across the moor with a wall on your left and after about 250m take the right fork downhill that leads to a wooden bridge. Cross the bridge and climb the hill with a wall on your left; and at the wall corner turn left, following the sign to Longshaw, again with a wall on your left.

D The path bears to the right away from the wall, climbing up on to the moor. The route then follows the concessionary path along White Edge for 2½km (1½ miles), initially staying on the top of the Edge, passing a trig point on your right and affording extensive views in all directions.

E The path arrives at a large crossing wall and, after passing through the wall, turns left and descends, with the wall on the left. As the wall disintegrates, the path turns steeply downhill to the right.

The Milestone, Curbar Gap

At the bottom of this short descent at a junction of paths, go straight ahead following the footpath sign to The Grouse Inn. This path passes through a gate in the tree line and then veers diagonally right to arrive at the road. Cross the road, turn left and walk downhill to pass The Grouse. Just past the building take the footpath signed on the right, cross the stile and walk downhill across three fields. Pass through a gateway, turn left and return to Haywood car park.

Millstone on Curbar Edge

THE HALLS WALK

After going through Holmesfield Park Wood, this walk provides excellent views over the upper Cordwell Valley and passes three historic local halls, Woodthorpe, Horsleygate and Fanshawe Gate.

DISTANCE	8¾km (5½ miles)
MINIMUM TIME	3 hours
TERRAIN	Good paths and field walking. No steep climbs
LANDSCAPE	Rolling farmland, wide valley views
START/FINISH	Fleur de Lys public house, Totley Hall Lane, Totley
PARKING	On-road parking on Totley Hall Lane
PUBLIC TOILETS	None on route
REFRESHMENTS	Fleur de Lys and Cross Scythes pubs in Totley, Angel Inn and the George & Dragon in Holmesfield
TRAINS & BUSES	Bus services 14, 97, 98, 213, 218, 293 and M17

Route Directions

A Walk down Totley Hall Lane, soon passing the School House on the left and Totley Hall Farm and Totley Hall on the right. Continue past Totley Hall Mead to the end of the road and over the stile. Take the public footpath on the left and follow the track, keeping the hedge on the left. Continue through the gate on the right and soon enter a wood (Gillfield Wood) and go for about 50m before taking a path to the left towards the wooden footbridge over the brook (Totley Brook).

B Pass over the stile and head uphill soon to emerge from the wood into a field. Now head uphill to the right of an evergreen coppice, which has a 'concealed' telecommunication mast within it. At the top of the field, it is worth turning to enjoy the wide view. Having crossed the stile that is just within the coppice, bear right keeping the stone wall on your left to pass the grounds of Woodthorpe Hall. **See Woodthorpe Hall**. Cross a further stile and then through a kissing gate and proceed to the road and turn right.

WOODTHORPE HALL: Woodthorpe signifies an outlying farm in a wood. Don't let yourself be beguiled by reference books: there is a part-medieval Woodthorpe Hall near Clay Cross. This one is 17th century and L-shaped. The Fanshawe family are believed to have built it after their old home at Fanshaw Gate was demolished, re-using the stone. There are three gables at the front and two at the side.

C After about 200m, and on a right hand bend in the road, take the footpath ahead through a wide gateway into Holmesfield Park Wood. **See Holmesfield Park Wood**. The wide footpath follows a straight line ahead through the wood to emerge at a field with a hedge on the right, where there are good views over Sheffield.

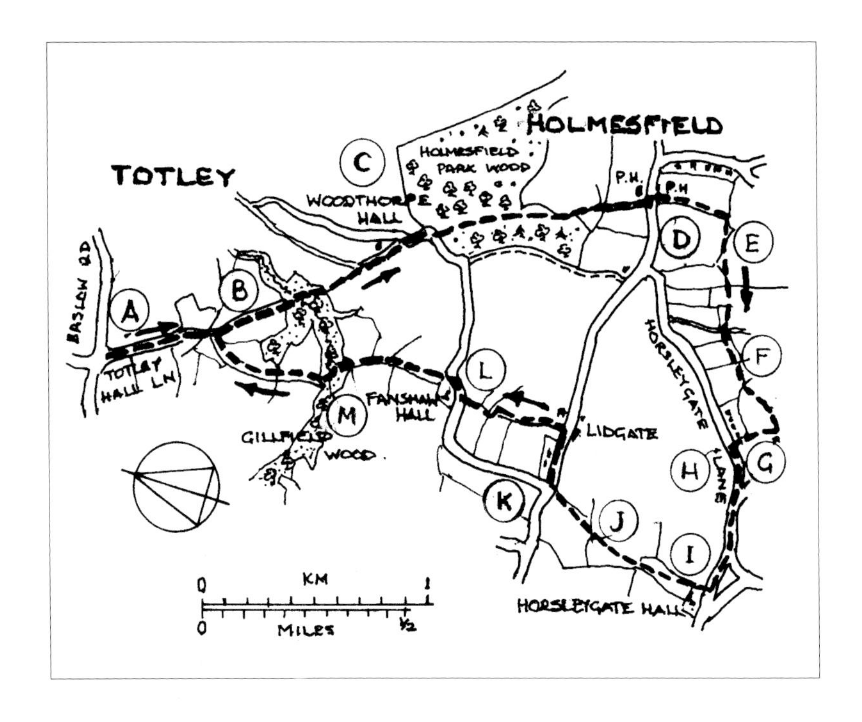

HOLMESFIELD PARK WOOD: Holmesfield Park Wood was once a deer park, owned in 1330 by the Deincourt family. As Mel Jones has shown, a likely memento of this is the ditch *inside* a section of the eastern bank, built to stop the deer escaping. Around 1600 it became a coppice wood (stumps cut to ground level). So along the opposite side the ditch is *outside* the bank which is topped with a stone wall, all to prevent farm animals from devouring the shoots from the stumps.

Continue ahead until the path meets a driveway to two houses. Again continue ahead to join the road by the side of the Angel Inn in Holmesfield.

D Taking care with the traffic, cross this road and turn left before walking to the George and Dragon public house. Immediately past the pub, turn right and follow the public footpath through a yard, across a stile and then downhill through the fields, with a wall and then a hedge on the right. A wide view of the head of the Cordwell valley faces you. After two more stiles, go straight ahead for 100 metres.

E Then, with a stile on your left, turn right and walk across a field, keeping a line of four individual trees on your left, to a stile and then continue ahead, with a hedge on your right, to another stile in a field corner. Continue ahead into the next field and cross a stile to the right of the field gate ahead of you. Head across the next field to a gate that takes you across a sunken lane. Continue ahead across fields. In the first you will pass through a line of trees; and in the second field you will have a hedge on your left until you arrive at a stile at the left of a facing wall.

F Bear directly ahead over the brow of the field ahead and then head down the slope, with a hedge on your right, to a stone squeeze stile in the right hand corner of the field. In the next field proceed diagonally right over the brow, descending to another stile in the lower right hand corner, which is immediately followed by a plank bridge over a ditch.

G Turn right up the steps and continue up the slope, with the stream on your right, to reach a small gate into the caravan park. Continue up the slope along the track between the caravans, always keeping directly ahead, and look ahead for a stile in the wall leading to the road (Horsleygate Lane). **See Horsleygate.**

HORSLEYGATE: The de Horseley family were here by 1388 and the Gate is mentioned in 1494. Kenneth Cameron thought it was probably one of the gates of the original Holmesfield Park. If so the park must have been a lot larger than the present Park Wood. Horsleygate Lane was part of a very old bridleway from Sheffield via Psalter Lane, Ringinglow Road, Thryft House, Whirlow Hall, Limb Lane, Dore, Old Hay, Totley and Holmesfield to the Baslow area.

H At the road, turn left to pass a large house, with a seat set within the stone wall at the entrance and house name stone *Horsleygate,* and continue downhill past Cordwell Barn on the right. **See Cordwell Barn.** Continue downhill until the road becomes level. Look next for a large holly bush on the right, immediately before the drive into Horsleygate Hall.

CORDWELL BARN: During conversion of the barn, a board listing toll charges was discovered. This, plus the curved outer wall of the building opposite {though straight inside), apparently made to facilitate transit, prompted a theory that the Barn was once a toll cottage. Unfortunately there is no record of any toll road here, though it was an ancient bridleway. On each end of the curved wall, at head height and depending on the light, the letter W is visible, reminiscent of a 16th-17th century device to ward off witches. It may, however, merely be the mark of the Wolstenholme family who lived at Horsleygate.

I This bush almost obscures the stile in the wall leading to a path uphill with a wall on your left. At the end of the wall cross a stone stile and head directly uphill to a wooden stile by a gorse thicket. Pass through the gorse thicket. Having dealt with this, continue uphill, keeping a fence and tree line over to your left.

J In the field after the one with the two derelict barns, bear diagonally to the right away from the wall and head towards the wall at the uppermost right hand end of the field. At the right hand end of this wall, where two walls join, is a stile. Continue into the next field and then pass to the left of a gorse thicket before reaching the road (Holmesfield to Owler Bar).

K Turn right here and cross the road when the traffic visibility is good. After about 400 metres, and immediately before a left hand bend in the road, you will arrive at Lydgate Cottage. **See Lidgate**. Immediately after this cottage, take the public footpath to the left signposted 'Fanshawe Gate for Totley', continuing ahead along the left hand field edges; and when you come to a point where the left hand field boundary fence diverges from the farmed field, keep next to the boundary fence.

LIDGATE: The name Lidgate comes from the Old English *hlid-geat,* a swing-gate. These were often erected at the edge of commons or greens to prevent animals from straying. This one is first recorded in 1693. In Dore the lane that subsequently became the top part of Dore Road, where there used to be a green, was known for centuries as Lidget Lane.

L After this point you will shortly arrive at a road (Fanshaw Gate Lane). **See Fanshawe Gate and Hall.** Here turn right to pass the entrances to both Fanshawe Gate House and Fanshawe Gate Hall and then follow the public footpath to the left signposted 'Totley 1 mile' along the driveway of the Old Hall, past the small pond before bearing right to a squeeze stile and then a stile leading to fields. Head downhill, keeping the field boundary on the left, before reaching a wood (Gillfield Wood).

FANSHAWE GATE AND HALL: This place has a curious history .The Fanshawes, minor gentry, lived here from about 1400 until1944. In the 16th-18th centuries they were courtiers, top men in the Exchequer. Local historians disagree about whether the old hall was dismantled before, during or just after the Civil War (1642-49). The present small manor house with its ornate gateposts soon replaced it. Two ancient outbuildings of two and four storeys may or may not have been part of the former hall.

M Enter the wood and cross the bridge before heading diagonally left up the slope to turn left on to a crossing path. After about 50m, turn right and head for a gate and stile combination. Continue ahead, keeping the hedge on the left, until the path meets a track. Turn right onto the track, which leads back to Totley Hall Lane.

Woodthorpe Hall

RIVER DERWENT AND FROGGATT EDGE

A walk combining views of the usually tranquil waters of the Derwent together with the invigorating blast of fresh air along Froggatt Edge - and the unmissable Grindleford Station cafe!

DISTANCE	9km (5½ miles)
MINIMUM TIME	3 hours
TERRAIN	Good paths and tracks, a stiff climb to Froggatt Edge
LANDSCAPE	River bank, woodland and edge walking
START/FINISH	Grindleford Station approach
PARKING	Grindleford Station approach
PUBLIC TOILETS	None on route
REFRESHMENTS	Grindleford Station cafe and Chequers Inn
TRAINS & BUSES	Train and bus services 65, 214 and 240

Route Directions

Before you set off, you might like to read the following about Padley Chapel, which you will shortly pass.

PADLEY CHAPEL: The sole surviving part of Padley Hall is the gatehouse, now used as a Roman Cathoic chapel and pilgrimage site. Sir Thomas Fitzherbert acquired Padley through marriage and leased it to his brother John. As a Catholic, Thomas was imprisoned in 1561. After Mary Queen of Scots was executed in 1587, there was a Spanish invasion scare. Catholics became even more suspect. In July 1588 a search party raided Padley and found two priests, Nicholas Garlick and John Ludlam. They, John Fitzherbert and his son Anthony were taken to Derby Gaol. The priests were tried, along with another, and hanged. Meanwhile the Armada was sailing up the Channel, to be harassed by the English fleet and defeated at the Battle of Gravelines. John Fitzherbert died in the Fleet Prison, London and Sir Thomas died in the Tower. Then Anthony recanted and recovered Padley, which had briefly been in the hands of Richard Topcliffe, the notorious inquisitor.

A Head down to the station, pass the cafe on your right and cross over the bridge, with Totley Tunnel on your right. Continue ahead on to the unmade road, signposted public footpath, crossing a bridge over a stream and then passing Padley Mill on your right. Keep ahead and soon pass Brunts Barn on your left and Padley Chapel on your right. Continue ahead until you reach a cattle grid.

Padley Chapel

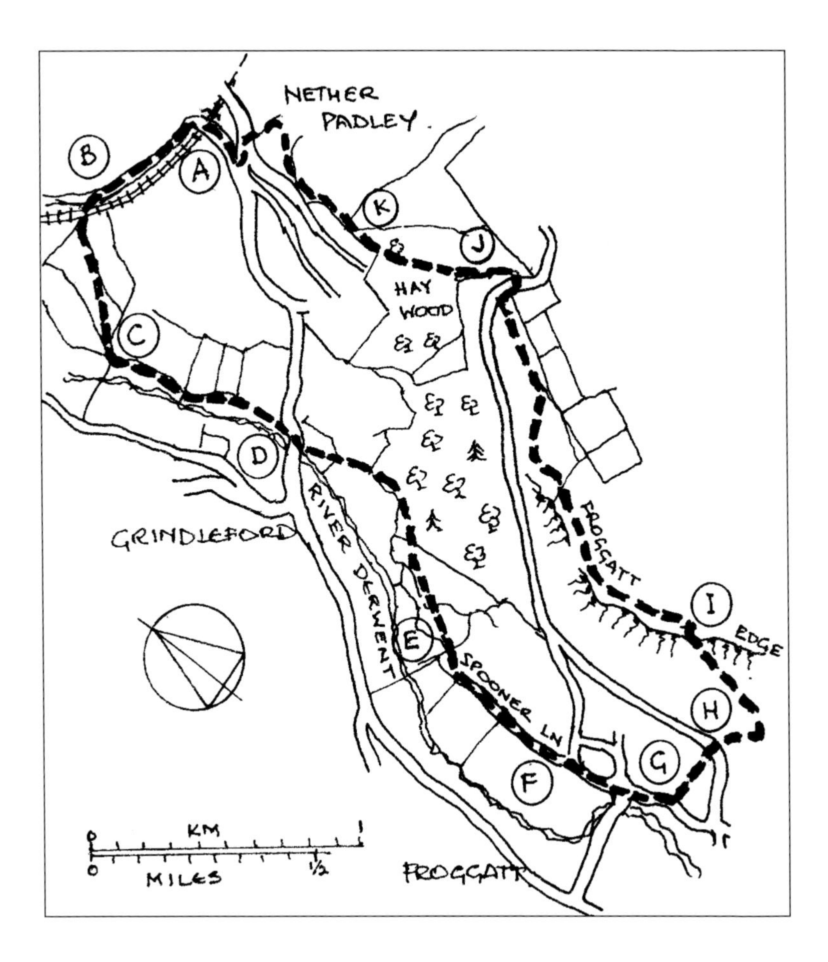

B Go over this and then turn left, go through a kissing gate and over the railway line. Now continue on the well-defined path for about 150m and then turn left through a gap in the wall by some old wooden gate posts. Then follow an indistinct path diagonally right across the field to the far right corner to another gap with stone gate posts. Turn left with the wall on your right, proceeding downhill until you reach a track at the bottom of the field.

C Turn left at the track,cross a bridge and then turn right to reach the riverbank. Follow the river to Grindleford. **See Grindleford.**

GRINDLEFORD: Grindleford Bridge was mentioned in 1577. The Buxton branch of the Sheffield and Chapel Turnpike (post 1758) crossed Houndkirk and descended via Fox House to Grindleford, continuing to Great Hucklow, Tideswell and beyond by way of Sir William Hill. This gentleman has been identified as Sir William Saville, 2nd Marquis of Halifax, a 17th century lord of Eyam manor. The toll house also caught the traffic to and from another branch turnpike from here via Bakewell to Newhaven on the Ashbourne-Buxton road.

Toll Bar Cottage, Grindleford

Go through a small gate onto the road opposite the church, cross the road and turn right towards the traffic lights. Toll Bar Cottage is on your right. Turn left through the gate by the traffic lights onto a public footpath signposted Froggatt, Curbar, Calver and Chatsworth.

D Go straight ahead across the field to cross a stream and then through a kissing gate. Turn right and continue to another gate with a wall on your right. Proceed ahead through a gap in another wall and enter Horse Hay Coppice. Follow the stone path over a stream and enter Froggatt Wood. Continue along the stone path, crossing several streams. Leave the wood behind you by passing through a stone stile into a field.

E Go directly ahead across the field, through another stile with a wall on your right, continuing with the wall on your right to reach another gateway. Go through a stile in the wall on the right and walk diagonally right to approach the right end of the wall ahead. Go round the wall as marked by a yellow arrow sign and proceed along the path with a wall on your left to another stile at the side of a gate. This leads into a walled track, which is partly paved with ancient stone slabs, which then becomes a tarmac lane (Spooner Lane) as you enter Froggatt.

F Turn right at the T-junction and continue down Hollowgate on the raised footpath, passing the road bridge on your right, and continue ahead on Froggatt Lane for about 160m.

G Turn left as indicated by the public footpath sign at the side of Meadowcroft. Follow the path to climb uphill through woodland to reach a stile. Climb over the wall and onto the main road below the Chequers Inn.

H Cross the road to a public footpath sign opposite and continue to climb on a path, first to the right then to the left. Part way up the climb pass through a wall and gate and continue uphill, steep in places and over boulders, to reach a track immediately below the Edge. Turn right and proceed below the rocks for 100m. Bear left and follow the track aiming for a wooden marker post at the top of the slope.

I You are now on Froggatt Edge. Turn left on the broad track and enjoy a level part of the walk with lovely views all around. Further along you pass a stone circle on the right. Continue ahead on the track passing through a gate and on to another gate which leads on to the main road.

J Turn right, walk for about 40m and cross to a public footpath signposted Longshaw Estate. Go through a gate and down steps to cross a stream and then up to pass through an opening in a wall, continuing uphill on a cobbled path. At a junction of paths take the left fork; at the next junction turn left again down to a gate. Go through the gate and follow a clear path through woodland. At a Y-junction, keep to the right hand, higher and wider path. Follow this, arriving at a gate by a sign informing you that you are leaving Haywood.

K The path ahead now has a wooden fence on its left, with gardens below, and emerges onto a private road. Turn right and walk to the end of the road to join the main road. Cross over, turn right and walk for about 30m. Turn left at a public footpath sign and walk downhill to arrive at the station approach alongside the Station Cafe.

GRINDLEFORD STATION: By the Dore & Chinley Railway Act of 1884, the Company was to build a passenger station at or near Grindleford Bridge. This was for the benefit of the Duke of Rutland. (The Duke of Devonshire secured a similar provision for Hathersage.) In the event, the nearest point was to be Upper Padley. Its situation is naturally dramatic, even more so when a train emerges from the tunnel.

An evening on Froggatt Edge

EYAM, CALVER AND FROGGATT BRIDGE

A circular walk that combines some typical White Peak country with a delightful stretch alongside the River Derwent. The attraction of Eyam, with its links to Dore, is a bonus.

DISTANCE 9½km (6 miles)
MINIMUM TIME 3 hours
TERRAIN Footpaths, tracks and lanes
LANDSCAPE Limestone upland and riverside
START/FINISH Eyam village centre
PARKING On road in village centre or car park about 500m away
PUBLIC TOILETS Eyam car park
REFRESHMENTS Plenty of choice in Eyam and at Calver
TRAINS & BUSES Bus services 65, 214 and 240

Route Directions

Before we start, a few words about the village. **See Eyam**

EYAM: For Eyam s history, look around you! Now consider its links with Dore. Thomas Stanley, rector William Mompesson s right-hand man during the Plague of 1665-6, had been curate of Dore c.1632-6, marrying a local woman, Mary Raworth. He was rector of Eyam for 18 years from 1644. Ejected, he returned, dying in 1670. Dore s famous schoolmaster Richard Furness was born (1791) and buried (1857) in Eyam. His family home still stands at Townhead (see board), his prominent grave is near the church tower.

A Leave the Town Square by Lydgate, to the right of Eyam Tea Rooms. Pass Mill Lane on the left, with the information board nearby, and continue ahead on the path signed to Boundary Stone and Stoney Middleton. After 700m, near the summit, is the Boundary Stone. Continue downhill on the path, passing a line of conical depressions on the right, where lead ore was mined. Reaching a tarmac lane, turn right downhill to meet a wider road. Turn right down to the main road (A 623) at an octagonal stone building. **See Stoney Middleton.**

STONEY MIDDLETON: Stoney Middleton had an important industrial past, with lime-burning and lead-smelting further up the dale, depicted in dramatic drawings by Sir Francis Chantrey. It also had thermal springs. In the 18th century Lord Denman built baths and a well-chapel with an unusual octagonal nave and lantern, now the church. The village, however, could not vie with Buxton. The octagon theme was repeated in the 1840 tollhouse, later a chip shop. The Hall is 16th or 17th century, considerably altered.

B Cross this road and go ahead up a signed, asphalted footpath, to meet a road, with a school on your left. Turn right, uphill, for 50m then left into Eaton Fold, initially metalled but soon becoming a track. Just after the track bends slightly right, go through a pair of large stone gateposts and immediately turn right on to a signed footpath with a wall on the right.

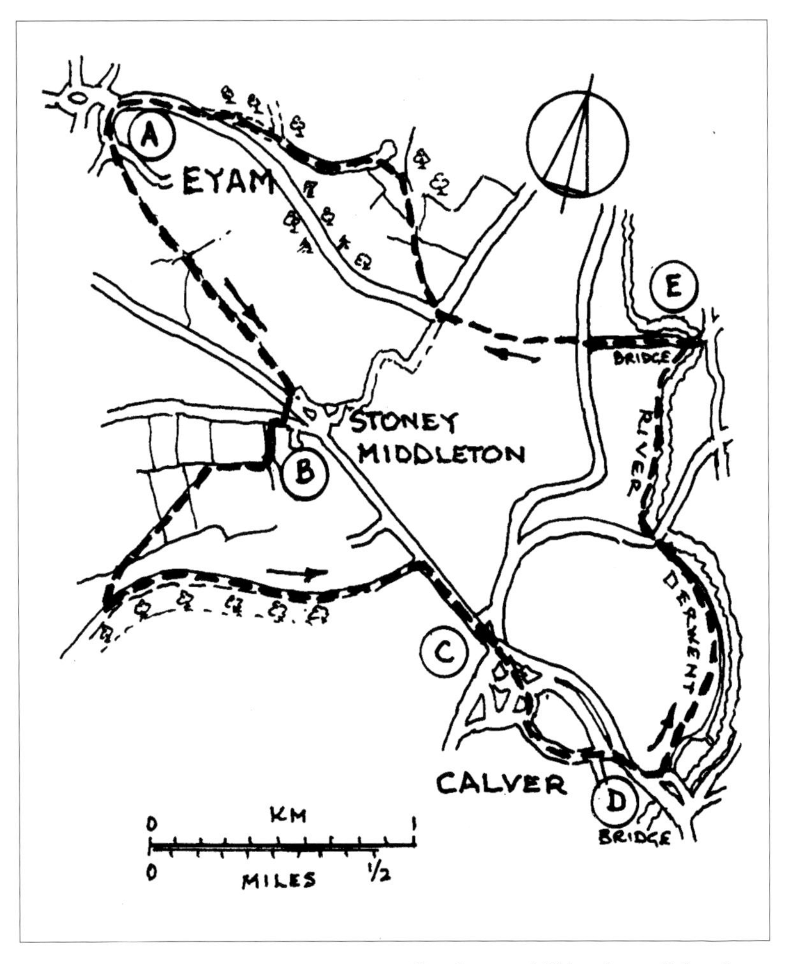

The Toll Bar, Stoney Middleton

Continue uphill by the wall for about 150m. As you approach the crest of the rise, go through a stile to the path junction and turn half left on to a path, signed Coombs Dale, over the field. At the 4th stone stile, enter scrubby woodland and go obliquely left down the hillside for about 250m to the valley bottom (Coombs Dale). Take care, as some parts are steep and slippery when wet. Cross a wooden stile and a stream to reach a roughly-metalled track.

Turn left and continue for 1300m (¾ mile) to meet a main road, near the recreation ground. Cross to the pavement, turn right and continue for 400m to the traffic lights at Calver cross roads. **See Calver.**

CALVER: Calver was once significant as an industrial centre, with lead-mining and cotton-spinning, now defunct, and as a transport hub, which it remains. It featured three branches of the Chesterfield and Hernstone Lane Head Turnpike (1759): from Bar Brook through Curbar Gap to Calver Bridge, Stoney Middleton and via its steep High Street to Wardlow Mires; from Calver Bridge to Baslow; and from Grindleford Bridge via Calver, Hassop, Bakewell, Conksbury and Friden to Newhaven on the Ashbourne-Buxton road.

C At this junction turn right, then immediately left into Sough Lane, on the right hand side of the Outside shop. Pass the Derwentwater Arms, where the road becomes Folds Head, and continue to the commemorative lamp at the three-way junction by the Post Office. Bear left here into Main Street and continue for about 450m, passing Calver Methodist Church on the left, to meet a main road, with a phone box on the right. Turn right and continue for about 100m before crossing the main road. Continue to the right and soon turn left on to the road leading to the old road bridge over the river (River Derwent).

D Just before the bridge, turn left on to a path signed New Bridge & Froggatt, initially along a metalled lane, with Calver Mill visible on the right. **See Calver Mill.**

CALVER MILL: At Calver Mill they, mainly women and children, spun cotton yarn, much of it for Leicester hosiery. John Gardom, a Bakewell merchant, and John Pares built the first mill in 1785 on a corn mill site. It burnt down in 1802 and was rebuilt. Cotton spinning finished in 1923. After the war, the mill became a factory making stainless steel sinks and starred in the TV series, *Colditz*.

Pass the private entrance to Calver Mill on the right and continue ahead past Stocking Farm, with its curved end wall and other unusual features, to the gate ahead leading into a field. This path soon goes alongside the leat, or goyt, that fed the water wheels at Calver Mill. Just after passing two cottages on the left, the path reaches a road (A625) on a bend.

Froggatt Bridge

Cross ahead here and down steps to continue with the river still on your right and passing some information boards. After about 100m, the path divides; bear right over the brook (Stoke Brook) via a bridge, spotting a brook lamprey, if you can, and continue for about 500m beside the river to the next bridge (Froggatt Bridge).

E Where the path meets the road, turn left and go about 400m gently uphill, passing Stoke Hall away on the right, to a T-junction at the B6001, Bakewell to Hathersage road. **See Stoke.**

Cross directly ahead and take the stile leading to a path up the field, continuing through a stile or adjacent gate, now with a wall on the right. At the road, cross and go just a few metres left before turning right through a stile, to an unsigned track going uphill with a wall on the right. Go through another gate ahead and continue uphill on a rutted track between gorse.

STOKE: Stoke was a detached part of the King s Hope estate even before 1066, so probably means a secondary settlement . In the 16th century it went through the hands of the famous Bess of Hardwick, who presented it to her son Charles Cavendish. Stoke Hall was built in 1757 for the Rev John Simpson. Pevsner calls it quite stately . The tollhouse (1759) was on the Grindleford-Newhaven branch turnpike. Stoke Hall Quarry provided the sandstone for Sheffield s Town Hall and Dore s Ecgbert Stone.

Turn left where the track meets another at a T-junction and continue through the edge of woodland (Stoke Wood) to meet a metalled lane. Turn left, gently downhill, and after 160m pass Riley Graves on the right. Continue down the lane, passing the Wesleyan Chapel on the left, back into Eyam Town Square.

Curbar Edge from the River Derwent

BIBLIOGRAPHY

In compiling the background items, help has been received from Sheffield Local Studies Library and from many printed sources, including in particular:

BALL, C., CROSSLEY, D. & FLAVELL, N. *Water Power on the Sheffield Rivers,* 2nd edn (South Yorkshire Industrial History Society, 2006)

BUXTON, B.A. *Hathersage in the Peak* (Phillimore, 2005)

CRAVEN, M. & STANLEY, M. *The Derbyshire Country House,* 2 vols (Landmark Publishing, 2001)

DERRY, J. (revd G.H.B. WARD). *Across the Derbyshire Moors,* 24th edn (Sheffield Telegraph & Star, 1946)

DODD, A.E. & E.M. *Peakland Roads and Trackways* (Moorland Publishing Co., 1974)

DUNSMORE, J. *Totley Rise Methodist Church 1896-1996* (the author, 1996)

DUNSTAN, J. *Dore Old School in Records and Recollections* (Dore Village Society, 2006)

The Origins of the Sheffield and Chesterfield Railway (Dore Village Society, 1970)

DUNSTAN, J. & MILLICAN, R. *The A to W of Dore* (Dore Village Society, 2002)

EDWARDS, B. *Drawings of Historic Totley* (Shape Design, 1979)

Totley and the Tunnel (Shape Design, 1985)

FROST, S. *Whirlow: The Story of an Ancient Sheffield Hamlet* (the author, 1990)

HARRIS, H. *Industrial Archaeology of the Peak District* (David & Charles, 1971)

HEY, D. *Packmen, Carriers and Packhorse Roads* (Landmark Publishing, 2001)

HULBERT, M.F.H. *Discovering Hathersage Old Vicarage* (Hathersage P.C.C., 1985)

JOHNSON, S. *A Short History of the Rifle Range at Totley, Sheffield* (the author, 1993)

JONES, M. *Sheffield's Woodland Heritage,* revd edn (Green Tree Publications, 1993)

NIXON, F. *Industrial Archaeology of Derbyshire* (David & Charles, 1969)

PEVSNER, N. *The Buildings of England: Derbyshire* (Penguin Books, 1953)

SMITH, H. *Turnpike Trail: Greenhill to Calver, Sheffield to Baslow* (the author, 1997)

Turnpike Trail: Sheffield to Chapel-en-le-Frith, 2nd edn (the author, 1995)

SMITH, T. *Historical Notes about Bradway,* revd edn (the author, 1999)

STRATFORD, J. *A History of Totley All Saints Church of England School, Sheffield, 1827-2000* (the author, 2000)

TURBUTT, G. *A History of Derbyshire,* 4 vols (Merton Priory Press, 1999)

YOUNG, B. & GARLAND, E., ed.y *From Dore to Dore: Some Local Walks* (Dore Village Society, 1973).

INDEX

Directly and indirectly historical references are in **bold** numbers.

E

F

G

H

I

J

K

L

M

S

T

U

V

W

Y